Research Studies in Library Science, No. 11

RESEARCH STUDIES IN LIBRARY SCIENCE
Bohdan S. Wynar, Editor

No. 1. *Middle Class Attitudes and Public Library Use.* By Charles Evans, with an Introduction by Lawrence Allen.

No. 2. *Critical Guide to Catholic Reference Books.* By James Patrick McCabe, with an Introduction by Russell E. Bidlack.

No. 3. *An Analysis of Vocabulary Control in Library of Congress Classification and Subject Headings.* By John Phillip Immroth, with an Introduction by Jay E. Daily.

No. 4. *Research Methods in Library Science. A Bibliographic Guide.* By Bohdan S. Wynar.

No. 5. *Library Management: Behavior-Based Personnel Systems. A Framework for Analysis.* By Robert E. Kemper.

No. 6. *Computerizing the Card Catalog in the University Library: A Survey of User Requirements.* By Richard P. Palmer, with an Introduction by Kenneth R. Shaffer.

No. 7. *Toward a Philosophy of Educational Librarianship.* By John M. Christ.

No. 8. *Freedom versus Suppression and Censorship.* By Charles H. Busha, with an Introduction by Peter Hiatt, and a Preface by Allan Pratt.

No. 9. *The Role of the State Library in Adult Education: A Critical Analysis of Nine Southeastern State Library Agencies.* By Donald D. Foos, with an Introduction by Harold Goldstein.

No. 10. *The Concept of Main Entry as Represented in the Anglo-American Cataloging Rules. A Critical Appraisal with Some Suggestions: Author Main Entry vs. Title Main Entry.* By M. Nabil Hamdy, with an Introduction by Jay E. Daily.

No. 11. *Publishing in Switzerland: The Press and the Book Trade.* By Linda S. Kropf.

Publishing in Switzerland

The Press and the Book Trade

Linda S. Kropf

1973

LIBRARIES UNLIMITED, INC., LITTLETON, COLO.

TABLE OF CONTENTS

LIST OF TABLES

To my husband
Daniel

LINGUISTIC MAP OF SWITZERLAND

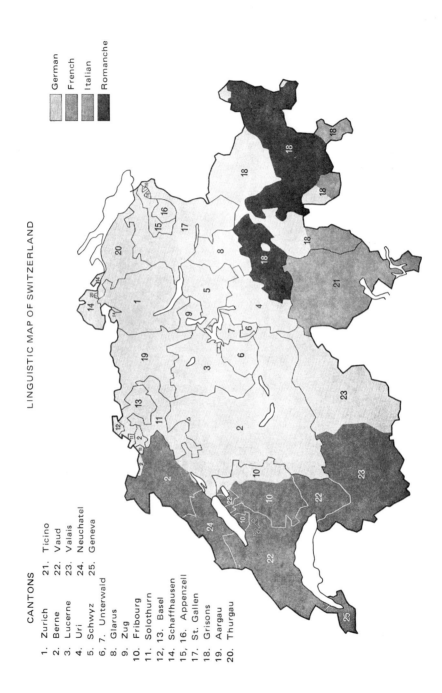

CANTONS

1. Zurich	21. Ticino
2. Berne	22. Vaud
3. Lucerne	23. Valais
4. Uri	24. Neuchatel
5. Schwyz	25. Geneva
6. 7. Unterwald	
8. Glarus	
9. Zug	
10. Fribourg	
11. Solothurn	
12, 13. Basel	
14. Schaffhausen	
15, 16. Appenzell	
17. St. Gallen	
18. Grisons	
19. Aargau	
20. Thurgau	

German
French
Italian
Romanche

Preface

Much has been written on the press and publishing in major countries, yet relatively little information is available on publishing in smaller nations. Switzerland, a multilingual nation, has a publishing sphere which is divided by language and culture, a situation which creates unique problems for the press and the book trade industry.

Switzerland, with her various cultures and peoples, has been of interest to me since I studied in this country as an undergraduate student in 1967. In December 1969, I returned to do research on the publishing situation for my Master's thesis in library science, and the foundation of this study evolved at this time. Most of the information was gathered through interviews, correspondence and questionnaires.

While living in Toronto in 1970, I attended Miss Francis Halpenny's course on Canadian publishing at the School of Library Science, University of Toronto. Some of the problems discussed reminded me of Swiss publishing difficulties.

I had the opportunity to expand and update my study on publishing early in 1972 when I moved to Zurich with my Swiss husband. In the process of collecting documents and interviewing, I became indebted to a large number of people—publishers, newspaper editors, librarians, and public servants—throughout Switzerland. I wish to thank all the people who helped me with their advice and encouragement. I had considerable assistance from Mr. Peter Oprecht of the Swiss Booksellers' and Publishers' Association, Mr. Paul Adler of Pro Helvetia, and Drs. F. G. Maier and Rätus Luck at the Swiss National Library in Bern. I also wish to thank Dr. Ivan Kaldor, Dean of the

PREFACE

School of Library and Information Science, State University of New York at Geneseo, for his help with my early research.

This study is divided into four major parts. Chapter 1 presents an historical survey of the development of multilingualism in Switzerland. In Chapter 2 the characteristics and language-related distribution patterns of the Swiss press are discussed, while the history and present state of Swiss book publishing are studied in Chapter 3. The directory portion of the study, listing publishing firms, is composed almost entirely of information gathered from questionnaires. No international organizations having publishing activities are listed, as this would be a whole project on its own, considering the number of international associations located in Switzerland. The listing of newspapers is arranged by city, as this seemed to be the most practical grouping; only cities with populations of 8,000 and over are included.

1

A Profile of Switzerland
as a Multilingual Nation

The central theme of Switzerland's history is that of unity despite great diversity. The country was not formed by such binding factors as common language, culture, or religion but on like political conviction. Switzerland is an *Eidgenossenschaft*, or confederation by oath. This small nation is not a uniform national state, nor has it ever aspired to be one. Indeed, the variety of its character and composition is a cherished tradition. The 22 cantons and three half cantons, made up of more than 3,000 communes, preserve their right to self-government that is the basis of Swiss democracy.

The Setting

Switzerland's contrasting regions and natural boundaries constitute geographical obstacles to unity. This landlocked country in the heart of Western Europe is surrounded on all sides by natural barriers: to the east and north by the Rhine River (as far as the city of Basel), then to the west by the Jura mountains; to the south by the forbidding peaks of the Alps and the waters of Lake Geneva. The southeastern portion of Switzerland is the only area which is free from a natural boundary. The canton of Ticino slopes into the plain of Lombardy in Italy and allows for easy access to the south.

Four countries which have historically been centers of power and aggression serve as Switzerland's neighbors. The existence of these countries played an important role in the creation of a unified confederation. Because of threats from these neighbors, Switzerland adopted permanent neutrality, to protect its very existence.

A PROFILE OF SWITZERLAND AS A MULTILINGUAL NATION

It was in the thirteenth century that the Swiss first formed a union to resist invasion and foreign rule. From this time, the history of the country has essentially been the history of cantonal development.[1] The cantons retain considerable autonomy, guaranteed under the Constitution.

The differences in language and religion can be clearly seen in the cantons. There are four national languages—German, French, Italian, and Romansch—spoken among the total population of over six million. Romansch, however, because of its relative obscurity, is not an official language, as the others are. The various language communities are located, with a few exceptions, in more or less contiguous areas within the country. There are sixteen cantons where German is the majority language; five cantons are predominantly French; and only one canton has an Italian language majority. The French-speaking community occupies the western cantons of Geneva, Vaud, and Neuchâtel and a part of the cantons of Valais, Fribourg, and Bern. The German-speaking community inhabits a larger share of the country— from the German-French boundary of the three cantons mentioned above (Valais, Fribourg, Bern) to the Austrian border, and from the foot of the Alps in the south to Lake Constance and the Rhine. A German-speaking majority is also found in the canton of Grisons in the southeastern part of Switzerland. The Swiss-Italian group is located in the canton of Ticino and in parts of the canton of Grisons. The Grisons or Graubünden is also the home of the Romansch-speaking group, numbering only 50,339 in 1970.[2]

The vast disparity in size of the four language groups is seen in the population statistics of these various communities. The last census of 1970 shows the language breakdown as follows: German speakers represent 74 percent of the population; French, 20 percent; Italian, 4 percent; and Romansch, scarcely 1 percent. These figures, however, do not include the important minority made up of foreign residents, who numbered over one million in 1970. The greatest portion of this group is made up of Italian workers attracted to Switzerland by the labor shortage and higher wages.

Origins of the People

The multilingual society which exists in Switzerland owes its origin as much to history as to geography. Switzerland's history begins

12

in the mountain areas rather than in the plains, where the greater portion of the population lives today. Hunters from the Lower Palaeolithic period are thought to have existed in Alpine caves at altitudes ranging from 4,500 to 6,500 feet above sea level. They retreated to lower levels during the Magdalenian period.[3]

Archaeologists have discovered evidence of Neolithic man particularly on the shores of the lakes in Switzerland. They are thought to have made log huts supported on piles on the lake shores. They fished and farmed in these lakeside settlements.

In the Bronze Age Switzerland's inhabitants depended on trade from the Mediterranean lands to bring them tin and copper to make bronze. In the later Iron Age, however, they were probably able to smelt iron ore in their own furnaces. It was during this time that the population began to increase in the plateau regions and in the Jura area.

The Celts migrated to the area we know today as Switzerland in the fifth century B.C. Gradually, the greater part of the country was occupied by the Helvetii who, for more than 500 years, were under the rule of Rome. Under the influence of the imperial city, the road system was extended and several large towns flourished. Soldiers, merchants, and officials came over the mountain passes bringing with them the language and culture of the Roman civilization. Roman domination is evidenced by the fact that three of Switzerland's national languages have Latin roots: French, Italian, and Romansch.[4]

The establishment in Switzerland of diverse cultural groups occurred as a result of the Germanic invasions in the fourth century A.D. Germanic Burgundians, who inhabited the western part of the country, were relatively few in number and soon became Romanized through contact with the local population. On the other hand, the invasion in the northeast by the more aggressive Germanic tribe, the Alemanni, had a decisive effect on the future of this region, which was to become German-speaking Switzerland.

The Latin language survived south of the Alps. The inhabitants of the canton of Ticino speak an Italian dialect of the Lombard group, originating from Latin. Latin was also the language in Rhaetii, where the Rhaeto-Romanic dialects developed. Only two of these dialects, Ladin and Romansch, became written languages and thrived during the Reformation. During the latter part of the Middle Ages, the Rhaeto-Romanic area extended north to Lake Constance and west to the St. Gotthard pass. Today Rhaeto-Romanic, or Romansch, exists only in the higher valleys of the Grisons in the southeast portion of Switzerland.

The areas inhabited by the Burgundians form what is known as *la Suisse romande*, or French Switzerland. Latin was spoken here but was eventually replaced by a group of Franco-Provençal sub-dialects. These patois existed until a century ago.[5] French is the common language of the region today.

The Germanic cultural area flourished as a result of the Alemanni settlement. Dialects also developed in this region but, unlike the Franco-Provençal dialects, these variations (approximately 26) of the German language still exist. "Schwyzertütsch," as these dialects are collectively called, differs from High German to such an extent that the written language has to be learned at school almost as a foreign language. The written language—High German—of the Swiss-German is therefore substantially different from the spoken language. The resistance to pan-Germanism and Nazi pressure during World War II also contributed to the continued survival of these dialects.[6]

Background of Language Harmony

Language tolerance and cultural coexistence in Switzerland have been admired by countries around the world, especially by those nations which are torn by linguistic and cultural conflict.

The Swiss nation was formed historically through the development, of mutual defense alliances designed to protect local independence of a group of heterogeneous communes. This concept of communal independence has much to do with the fact that there is language equality in Switzerland today.[7]

The commune enjoyed a great deal of local autonomy. Laws were determined by the territorial principle, which also applied to the language of the commune. The local administration or authority would make a decision concerning what language should be used for the legal, administrative, and juridical affairs of the commune. When a communal territory was bordered by a different language group, one language was chosen as the "communal" tongue. Natives from other linguistic groups were therefore forced to learn the communal language and assimilate themselves in the new cultural environment. This territorial principle is still retained today in the cantons.

Exceptions to this strict language rule were found in areas

where economic growth had brought together people of various linguistic backgrounds. The most well-known examples are the towns of Biel/Bienne and Sierre/Siders, both of which are located on the German-French frontier. It was necessary and inevitable that there would be official recognition of the two languages represented in the towns. The citizens required that their language be respected by the government authority. Representative language groups had a "language right" in these particular areas and linguistic differences were tolerated without conflict.[8]

This practice of assimilation and recognition of language groups was brought on gradually before the days of the Reformation, when Switzerland was basically a German nation. The groups of French, Italian, and Romansch-speaking inhabitants who lived in the lands surrounding what was then Switzerland were associated with the Confederation during the sixteenth century only by treaty as allies. These areas were the Grisons, Valais, the principality of Basel and Neuchâtel, and the Republic of Geneva. The Vaud lands, Ticino, and parts of the present-day German Switzerland were governed as protectorates by one or more cantons. The ruling cantons respected the local autonomy of each region they ruled and observed tolerance for their language choice. These events occurred long before the nineteenth century, when the rest of Europe was so greatly concerned with the ideas of the unilingual national state.

To a large extent the national equilibrium found in Switzerland today owes much to the balance of demographic factors. There has been little migration, and on the whole the linguistic composition of the population has changed little during the last century.[9]

Linguistic divisions do not correspond to religious loyalties; in fact, both cut across cantonal boundaries. For example, in the canton of Zurich, where the majority language is German, Protestants outnumber Catholics. Lucerne, a strongly Catholic area, is also in the German-speaking part of the country. These religious differences have worked to offset the linguistic divisions. Historically, religion rather than language provoked conflict and problems in Switzerland.

The 22 cantons and three half cantons are "sovereign" in many respects, as guaranteed by Article 3 of the Federal Constitution. The cantons have a right to determine any language matters in their territory that are not governed by the Federal Constitution. In this way the cantons are able to preserve their linguistic character against all outside forces which may endanger it.

A PROFILE OF SWITZERLAND AS A MULTILINGUAL NATION

Today there is only one major exception to the peaceful coexistence among language groups. This is the Jura question, centered in the canton of Bern. There is a relatively active separatist movement in the French Jura area of the canton. This has been limited to a fairly small extremist group called "Front de Libération Jurassienne," which has committed scattered acts of violence to emphasize its campaign to separate from German-speaking Bern and form its own canton. In keeping with the tradition of favorable treatment for minorities, many Swiss-Germans feel that if the Jurassiens want a separate canton they should be allowed to have it. Most Swiss-French, on the other hand, have a less tolerant view of the situation and anticipate economic and practical problems in the formation of a new canton. It seems likely that the question will eventually be settled by Bern itself, following the tradition of cantonal autonomy.[10]

The Role of the Federal Government
in the Recognition of Swiss Languages

The linguistic situation in Switzerland becomes particularly apparent at the federal level of government. Although this may appear to be a difficult problem, in practice the legal regulation is quite simple. The main provision is contained in Article 116 of the Federal Constitution, which views German, French, and Italian as the "official" languages of Switzerland. In 1938, however, Romansch was recognized as the fourth "national" language. According to Mario M. Pedrazzini, a Swiss spokesman on the problem of languages in the Swiss federal government, the intention of this act was "to stress the political and cultural importance of the Latin element in the Confederation, without at the same time further complicating the functioning of the administrative apparatus. It constitutes in any event an explicit affirmation of the essential role of the different nationalities in the structure of the Swiss state."[11]

The recognition of Romansch as the fourth national language established the facts that the Swiss nation is made up of people from different language communities and that each group is an integral part of the country as a whole. In addition, the inclusion of Romansch as a national language shows the Swiss policy of toleration and acceptance of minority languages. The executive branch, or *Kleiner Rat*, of the canton of Grisons began to form plans to request a constitutional amendment to recognize Romansch in 1935. The promoters of this amendment never sought official language status for Romansch. They realized that this would involve the allocation of new funds for the translation of government documents and proclamations. What they did want was a firm declaration of the principle of a fourth language, mainly to strengthen the preservation of this ancient form of speech. Another event which propelled the movement to recognize Romansch was the Fascist claim in Italy that Romansch dialects were forms of Italian.[12] In 1937 the federal executive approved the proposal of the canton of Grisons and recommended the constitutional amendment to the federal parliament. There was some skepticism that the Swiss voters would find this a necessary addition to the Constitution. However, the voters proved that they realized this amendment was important to the Romansch-speaking group by accepting it by a 92 percent overall majority and by majorities in every canton.[13]

Thus, Romansch was accepted as the fourth "national" language. The distinction between official languages and national languages is that the former have certain rights in the parliamentary, administrative, and judicial spheres of the federal government while only a few basic laws are translated into Romansch: the Civil Code, the Code of Obligation, and the Penal Code. The translation expenses were underwritten at the combined expense of the federal and Grisons governments after the popular vote to sanction them.[14]

Trilingualism prevails in the two houses of the Federal Assembly, which use all three languages for debate and negotiation. In practice, however, a speech in Italian is rare, mainly because few members of the Federal Assembly understand Italian but also because the Swiss-Italian members can without difficulty express themselves in either German or French. Transactions between the cantons and branches of the federal government are conducted in the language of the individual canton. The use of the three predominant languages is important in Switzerland since the concept of direct democracy requires the citizen himself to make decisions about the laws. Therefore, it is significant that the official languages are equivalent in the voting process—for example, in the filling out of ballots—and that the official record appears in three languages.[15]

In addition to Article 116 the only other formal linguistic provision in the Federal Constitution appears in Article 107.[16] This article requires that the Federal Tribunal, or Supreme Court, should include representatives of the three major language groups. The

Confederation also works in various ways for the retention of "minority safeguards." Every year, sums of money are allocated to the preservation and furtherance of the cultural and linguistic individuality of the Italian and Romansch groups in the cantons of Ticino and Grisons. Pro Helvetia, a publicly authorized and federally funded organization, also works for the minority cause. This organization is devoted to the promotion of the cultural life of Switzerland and in particular to the cultural individuality of the linguistic minorities. Writing for Pro Helvetia, Carl Doka offers an interesting summary of the concept of minority safeguards: "Neither the linguistic minority nor the linguistic majority like to speak of 'minority safeguards.' The minority does not wish to be 'safeguarded' but respected, and the majority must not abuse its numerical superiority. The majority, in particular, must remain aware of the fact that the four national languages, and with them the four cultures emanating from them, are essential to what we understand as Switzerland."[17]

Language in the Schools

There is no National Department of Education in Switzerland. Education is basically a cantonal matter; there are 25 different educational systems. In some cases, notably Basel and Geneva, the cantons leave educational matters in primary schools up to the communes.[18]

The language of instruction generally follows the principle of territoriality. The process of assimilation of Swiss from other language areas is accomplished primarily through the schools.[19] In bilingual communities two school systems exist side by side to provide for both language groups.

Federal laws intervene into the realm of education only occasionally in order to aid primary schools and to provide subsidies for the weaker language groups. The legislative basis for this assistance is Article 27 *bis* of the Federal Constitution, which allows for the allocation of federal funds to the cantons for the support of primary education. An amendment to this law in 1953 allows for an annual grant for every child between the ages of seven and fifteen. In addition to these funds, nine rural "mountain" cantons receive a supplementary payment for each student on account of their limited resources. The cantons of Ticino and Grisons are included in this group. These two cantons are singled out again to receive a second "linguistic supplement" to deal with the payment of textbooks and teacher training. The canton of Grisons receives slightly more funds per child in order to help deal with the difficulties of having six different languages and dialects represented in its school systems.[20]

Students in high schools or secondary schools are required to learn a second national language. Only about a third of the cantons require language instruction of the other Swiss languages at the elementary level. French is generally taught in the German and Italian parts of Switzerland while German is studied in *la Suisse romande*. Often, English or Italian is offered in the upper grades of secondary schools along with the classical languages of Latin or Greek. Students in the Italian-speaking part of the country are required to study three national languages.[21]

Most cantons believe that students should receive complete instruction in their own language before they begin to study one of the other national languages. Swiss-German children have the additional problem of mastering High German after having learned to speak only in "Schwyzertütsch." In some ways this proves to be a benefit to them since they learn the rudiments of studying a foreign language at a very early age. Many Swiss-Germans do become bilingual or even multilingual, although this may be attributed to the contact they have with other language groups and to their ease in assimilating themselves in foreign language communities, rather than to effective language instruction in the schools. Although the French-speaking Swiss study German at school, they rarely acquire the competency in this language that the Swiss-Germans show in speaking French. This phenomenon will be discussed in more detail later on.

The Italian-speaking Swiss, on the other hand, usually manage to master German or French and sometimes both. There are no Italian language universities in Switzerland, so the student must learn at least one of the other official languages if he intends to seek a university degree. Often, Swiss-Italians will concentrate on German rather than French since the German language universities in Switzerland are closer to their native canton. Before World War II, many Swiss-Italians went to Italy for their university education, but this trend has not yet been restored.

The Romansch areas constitute an exception to the rule that primary and secondary education are conducted in the language of the canton. The Romansch language is only used for the first three or four years in the school. German is the language of instruction for the remainder of the school years. After this switch to German, Romansch becomes merely a subject of study. Some Romansch communities commence with German from the start, although most Romansch areas have Romansch-speaking kindergartens for children below compulsory school age. Some Romansch-speaking Swiss are concerned about the exclusion of their language from the schools, mainly because of their worry over the survival of the language itself.[22]

There are seven universities in Switzerland, three in the German part of the country (Basel, Bern, Zurich) and three in the French-speaking area (Geneva, Lausanne, Neuchâtel), leaving Fribourg as the only bilingual university in the country. These are all controlled by their respective cantons. Only the Federal Institutes of Technology at Zurich and Lausanne are federally supported.[23]

Linguistic Interaction

The individuality of each language group, which is very apparent in Switzerland, is a concept that amazes most visitors to the country. Surrounding this formulation is the widespread use of dialects, particularly in the German-speaking areas of Switzerland. The Swiss-German, regardless of his class or level of education, prefers to speak "Schwyzertütsch" rather than High German. There is no feeling of inferiority connected with the use of "Schwyzertütsch." Swiss-Germans are emotionally attached to their dialect and always use it in everyday conversation. The communities in the German-speaking area cling to their dialects in order to preserve a certain sense of individuality, not only against Austria and Germany but even against each other. For example, the Zurich dialect differs substantially from the Basel form of "Schwyzertütsch." The dialect is discarded only at formal occasions, at conferences, or on television and radio in order to allow for uniformity when different dialect groups are involved.

There are two principal dialects of the Romansch-speaking community: Surselvic, in the upper valley of the Rhine, and Ladin, in the Lower Engadine. Other forms of Romansch between these two points are distinct enough to necessitate the publication of elementary school books in four different variations of this language.[24]

The existence of various dialects is almost unknown in the

Italian and French areas. Some Swiss-Italian residents in the canton of Ticino speak Lombard dialects, but standard Italian is increasingly supplanting these local patois. The French spoken in *la Suisse romande* is almost identical with Parisian French, although there are minor differences.

There is a widespread misconception abroad that all Swiss are exceptional linguists and speak not only the four national languages but English as well. It is probably true that a large percentage of Swiss do know at least one foreign language, but there are no official statistics measuring bilingualism. Many Swiss find it essential to know two or three languages as a prerequisite for their chosen occupation, especially those people involved in tourism, commerce, or finance. Employees for the railroad, postal, and telephone system must be competent in French and German. Another factor which encourages bilingualism is marriage between people of two different language backgrounds. This is not an uncommon event in Switzerland, considering the close proximity of the various language groups. Intermarriages between French and German groups are the most common, followed by German-Italian inter-marriages.

The French-German relationship in all phases of Swiss life is by far the most important. Whenever a French-speaking Swiss and a Swiss-German meet, their conversation will almost always be in French, even though both parties may be perfectly bilingual. This is also true in written correspondence. One reason for this tendency is that frequently Swiss-Germans prefer to speak French rather than High German. It is also generally true that the French-speaking Swiss avoid speaking German if at all possible. The French language has a certain amount of prestige in Switzerland and Swiss-Germans are often eager to practice speaking this language, therefore making it unnecessary for most French-speaking Swiss to make any attempt at German.

History can help to explain the foundation of French as a prestigious language. French was the language of the ruling aristocracies in many Swiss-German cantons from the seventeenth century onwards. French has always been thought of as the language of diplomacy and it is often used in international organizations. The Swiss-Germans feel a strong need to learn French and often follow the pattern of a *Welschlandjahr*, or a sojourn to *la Suisse romande*, in order to immerse themselves in the French culture and language. Few French-speaking Swiss travel to the German part of the country because of the widespread use of Swiss-German dialects. Instead, they may go to Austria or Germany in order to learn High German.[25] However, there is not the same amount of eagerness on the part of the Swiss-French to learn German as there is on the part of the Swiss-German to master French. Most French-speaking Swiss never reach fluency in German.

The other minority languages in Switzerland are not of the same status as French. Relatively few French- or German-speaking Swiss learn Italian, and virtually no other Swiss learn Romansch. Both of these minority groups find that they must learn at least one of the other national languages. People from these language groups are therefore inevitably bilingual and often multilingual. It is safe to assume that a greater percentage of the Italian and Romansch-speaking Swiss are bilingual than either the Swiss-Germans or the Swiss-French.

From a cultural standpoint, Switzerland's three official languages all have roughly an equal status on the Continent. Each linguistic group in Switzerland is closely linked in cultural life to its neighboring nation.[26] Only the Romansch language is indigenous to Switzerland alone. Switzerland's affiliation with its neighbors is apparent in the varied literary tradition which the Swiss support. A Swiss student will study French, German, or Italian literature as his own. Only in the political and social sphere can one say that the Swiss show a kind of nationalism. The Swiss are brought together by their common belief in strong local autonomy, in decentralized federalism, and in the exercise of direct democracy, and by such institutions as the non-professional citizen army.

Although Swiss are culturally linked with their closest European neighbors, they share what Dr. Kenneth D. McRae calls a political culture.[27] The Swiss, no matter how influenced by their bordering nations, retain an outlook that is undeniably Swiss.

FOOTNOTES

1. Georg Thürer, *Free and Swiss* (London: Oswald Wolff, 1970), p. 12.

2. *Annuaire Statistique de la Suisse* (Bern: Bureau Fédéral de Statistique, 1972), p. 40. (All population statistics are taken from this source.)

3. Olivier Reverdin, *Introducing Switzerland* (Lausanne: Swiss Office for the Development of Trade, 1967), p. 9.

4. Thürer, *Free and Swiss*, p. 16.

5. Reverdin, *Introducing Switzerland*, p. 10.

6. *Ibid.*

7. Kurt Mayer, "Cultural Pluralism and Linguistic Equilibrium in Switzerland," *American Sociological Review*, April 1951, p. 157.

8. Carl Doka, "Switzerland's Four National Languages" (Zurich: Pro Helvetia, 1970), p. 5.

9. Mayer, "Cultural Pluralism and Linguistic Equilibrium in Switzerland," p. 158.

10. Kenneth D. McRae, *Switzerland: Example of Cultural Coexistence* (Toronto: Canadian Institute of International Affairs, 1964), p. 61.

11. Mario M. Pedrazzini, "The Linguistic Problem," in *Switzerland Present and Future* (Bern: The Yearbook of the New Helvetic Society, 1963), p. 179.

12. McRae, *Switzerland*, p. 9.

13. *Ibid.*

14. *Ibid.*

15. Pedrazzini, *Switzerland Present and Future*, p. 180.

16. McRae, *Switzerland*, p. 10.

17. Carl Doka, "Switzerland's Four National Languages," p. 11.

18. Eugène Egger, "L'Enseignement en Suisse" (Zurich: Pro Helvetia, 1971), p. 7.

19. McRae, *Switzerland*, p. 37.

20. *Ibid.*, p. 39.

21. *Ibid.*

22. *Ibid.*

23. Egger, "L'Enseignement en Suisse," p. 37.

24. McRae, *Switzerland*, p. 16.

FOOTNOTES

25. *Ibid.*, p. 18.

26. Paul Zinsli, *Vom Werden und Wesen der mehrsprachigen Schweiz* (Bern: Verlag Feuz, n.d.), Series: Schriften des Deutschschweizerischen Sprachvereins No. 1, pp. 30-34. Zinsli analyzes the special relationship each Swiss language group has with its respective neighboring countries. He reveals that there were variations in the intensity of these relations throughout history and shows that actions taken by Italy, Germany and, to some degree, France were not always in the best interest of the members of the various linguistic communities in Switzerland.

27. McRae, *Switzerland*, p. 21.

2

The Press: Diversity and Change

Switzerland has the greatest density of newspapers in terms of the number of published newspaper titles per capita. There is one paper to every 12,000 inhabitants. Approximately two-thirds of the papers are published in areas with fewer than 10,000 people. Today, there are 507 newspapers (of which one quarter are dailies), distributed in 285 cities and towns.[1]

The low circulation of individual papers illustrates the concept of decentralization that is so prevalent in all aspects of Swiss society. Today, the press as a whole reflects the linguistic variety, political character, and federative structure of the Confederation. A structural change, however, is taking place in the press due to the advent of popular papers and to changes in Swiss society. These trends toward concentration of the press and the implications of this formulation will be discussed in this chapter. To fully understand the radical changes that are occurring in the press, it is necessary to examine the characteristics and current state of the Swiss press.

Present Structure of the Swiss Press

The present diversified structure of the Swiss press is due largely to the fact that four languages are spoken in the country; the topographical factors, resulting in the organization of the country into small units, also contribute to the diversity of the press. These two factors, along with the federative structure of the country, have profoundly influenced Switzerland's cultural, religious, and industrial development as well as the development of the press.

Because of the profusion of newspapers in Switzerland, an estimated 50 percent have circulations of less than 5,000. Many of these papers are privately owned and, because of their small size and disparity, approximately half of them are losing money. Some depend on the profits of their commercial printing presses to make up for the papers' deficits.[2]

Regionalism, local civic feeling, and linguistic differences have helped to augment the decentralization evident in the Swiss press. Traditionally the Swiss have not been very mobile. Many do not move from their place of origin. The average Swiss is interested in local affairs and reads the local paper. In many cases, he will supplement his local paper with a general information daily which will give him further national and international news.[3] Local and regional news is an essential ingredient in all Swiss newspapers, even in those that have acquired an international audience. Those newspapers that wish to extend their readership beyond the town or city in which they are published often emphasize the local news in those areas in which they hope to gain subscribers.

A national press, dealing with national problems and having national distribution, is non-existent in Switzerland. Virtually all Swiss papers—apart from one exception which will be discussed later—cater to a local or regional readership rather than a national audience.

Even *Neue Zürcher Zeitung*, Switzerland's internationally known paper, never forgets to emphasize the local Zurich news. The *Tages-Anzeiger*, also based in Zurich, is the second largest paper in the country in terms of circulation rates, but it is rarely read outside Eastern Switzerland.[4] In *la Suisse romande*, *La Suisse* has expanded its circulation rate in the last few years to include subscribers outside its cantonal border, but it still accommodates space for news about Geneva and environs.

The present press structure has also been profoundly affected by the linguistic differences that are present in the Confederation. There is a close correlation between the number of newspapers in each language area and the population figures of these groups. Each language group supports a press close to the strength of its physical number (see Table I).

Papers printed in a dialect, such as in Swiss-German or in the Romansch varieties, are generally rare. *Nebelspalter*, a satirical weekly, occasionally has entire articles written in "Schwyzertütsch," but usually only captions to cartoons or other satirical matter is printed in this German dialect.[5]

PRESENT STRUCTURE OF THE SWISS PRESS

TABLE I

NEWSPAPERS CLASSIFIED BY LANGUAGE
(COMPARED TO POPULATION FIGURES)

Language	Newspapers†	in %	Population §	in %
German	370	73.0	3,864,684	74.4
French	111	21.9	1,045,091	20.1
Italian	22	4.3	207,557	4.0
Romansch	3	0.6	49,455	0.9
(Other languages)			(22,920)	
Total	506*		5,189,707	
Resident Population, including foreigners —			6,269,783	

*In addition, one paper is in Spanish, bringing the total to 507.

Source:

†Catalogue de la presse Suisse, 1972, Association d' Agences Suisses de Publicité, Zurich.

§Annuarie Statistique de la Suisse, 1972, p. 40. (Only Swiss citizens are tabulated.)

Bilingual newspapers are also a rarity, due to the high cost of printing. In the late 1950s there was a bilingual paper in Biel/Bienne, a town where two-thirds of the population speak German and one-third speak French. This publication disappeared, however, because everyone in the town was bilingual and could read in either language.[6]

The only bilingual newspaper that exists now is the *Fögl Ladin*, a small paper published in Samedam in the Engadine valley. This publication is printed in two variant types of Romansch, showing that the dialects are different enough to merit the inclusion of both forms in one paper. This paper, with a total circulation of 3,155 copies in the canton of Grisons, is of quite limited influence.

THE PRESS: DIVERSITY AND CHANGE

Within the category of daily papers, German-language newspapers show an indisputable leadership in publication figures. German
dailies represent 78.7 percent, while only 16.5 percent are printed in
French and 4.7 percent are in Italian. None of the Romansch papers
appear daily.[7]

Among the dailies having a circulation of more than 50,000,
eight are German, while four are French (see Table II). Only three
newspapers appear more than once a day with different editions and
these are all published in German Switzerland: *Basler Nachrichten*
(11 weekly); *National-Zeitung* (12 weekly); and *Neue Zürcher Zeitung*
(12 weekly).

TABLE II

LEADING DAILIES
(Over 50,000 Circulation)

German-Language Papers	French-Language Papers
Blick	Feuille d'Avis de Lausanne
Tages-Anzeiger	La Suisse
Neue Zürcher Zeitung	Tribune de Genève
National-Zeitung	Tribune-Le Matin
Berner Tabglatt	
Luzerner Neueste Nachrichten	
Vaterland	
Der Bund	

Source: **Catalogue de la presse Suisse, 1972.**

Sunday morning editions are almost non-existent in German
Switzerland. The *Berner Tagblatt* is the only German paper that
publishes a Sunday morning edition and its circulation is limited to
55,679 copies. In *la Suisse romande*, two papers publish a Sunday

morning edition: *La Suisse* and *La Tribune de Lausanne (Tribune-Dimanche)*, each selling in the area of 110,000 copies.[8]

Weekend and second or third editions are being additionally limited by reductions in the number of mail deliveries offered by the Post Office, which is the main source of distribution. Some of the major papers are bringing out their end of the week editions on Friday evening. During the week, a few papers have been forced to move up their afternoon editions to the morning. Some publishers fear that differences between papers will tend to be eliminated since all papers will cover basically the same news.

The news agencies in Switzerland reflect the multiformity that is present in the press structure. The major news agency is Agence Télégraphique Suisse ATS (SDA in German), founded in 1895. It is a joint-stock company financed and run by the Swiss press. The ATS is independent of the government and receives no subsidies from either the government or business. Some of its foreign news arrives via Swiss correspondents, but the majority of information is obtained by way of exchanges between foreign agencies, mainly Reuters and AFP. A total of 175 Swiss newspapers subscribe to the services of ATS: 62 German-language papers, 22 French-language, and six Italian-language papers.

In addition to ATS, Schweizerische Politische Korrespondenz serves small and medium-sized papers. It takes an active part in molding public opinion although it is not tied to any political party. Approximately 20 to 30 Swiss papers subscribe to United Press International, which has its head office in Zurich. It has to compete with the other foreign agencies (Associated Press, Reuter's Ltd., AFP, and Tass) that have offices in Switzerland.[9]

Political life within the Swiss system of direct democracy has greatly affected the evolution of a decentralized press in Switzerland. The Swiss have taken full advantage of the opportunities offered them by Switzerland's natural conditions and have invented a political system that has its roots in local units. It is here that popular opinion takes form and the political machinery commences.

The commune is the ideal sphere for the exercise of direct democracy. The Swiss assembled together are able to exert legislative power without an intermediary. The *Landsgemeinde*, or plenary assembly, stands for the purest and most direct democracy.[10]

All Swiss in the *Landsgemeinde* cantons and in the larger communities have the duty of electing a council and usually several other political bodies. They are also directly involved through the referendum system in all major policy decisions. In the elections the Swiss citizen votes as a supporter of a party, but in a referendum he votes as an individual expressing his own viewpoint about a particular measure.[11] It is for this reason that the Swiss believe that this type of democracy is absolutely unthinkable without a reliable, decentralized press. Even today, in the era of mass communications, many Swiss think that no other media can substitute for the press in bringing news and formulating opinions in the Swiss society.[12]

Public opinion in an individualistic sense is vital in a direct democracy where the citizen shapes the national will. In contrast to many other nations founded on a democratic structure, there is no definable and overwhelmingly influential public opinion in Switzerland. Multilingualism and the federative structure of the country have been instrumental in the development of a number of public opinions rather than one.[13]

Opinion Press and Politics

Historically the opinion or political press in Switzerland developed during the middle of the nineteenth century. During this period, political parties were founded in conjunction with the development of direct democracy. Printers and publishers, who were often politicians themselves, created their own papers to support their views. From this point on the political press grew until it became a big power. Only recently this press began to falter while the neutral or independent papers increased in number and circulation.[14]

In any case, the opinion press in Switzerland can still boast the greatest number of papers. More than 75 percent of all Swiss dailies fall into this category, along with a variety of weekly and semi-weekly newspapers.

Table III shows that liberal and radical papers lead in number although their circulation rates remain low. The radical press predominates in German Switzerland while the liberal press is mainly centered in the French-speaking part of the country. The most well-known Swiss paper, *Neue Zürcher Zeitung* (96,116), faithfully follows the opinions of the Radical Party (which is not really radical by American standards). It is well qualified in the areas of finance, economics, and international affairs and is in high esteem for its

30

TABLE III

POLITICAL ORIENTATION OF NEWSPAPERS

	Total Number
*Radical and Liberal	77
Catholic, Conservative	61
Socialist	17
Peasant, Artisan and Bourgeois	8
Communist	3

*The radical and liberal papers are tabulated together as indicated in the **Catalogue de la presse Suisse.**

excellent reporting. The *National-Zeitung* of Basel (80,463) is also associated with the Radical Party (or one of its branches) although it does not tenaciously rely on the official party line. Other influential papers among the radical press include: *Der Bund* of Bern (51,656), the *Luzerner Tagblatt* (23,615), the *St.-Galler Tagblatt* (45,577), the *Aargauer Tagblatt* (26,909), and the *Thurgauer Zeitung* (19,113). Most of these papers keep their distance from the party and feel free to stray from the official political outlook.

The *Gazette de Lausanne* (25,955) and the *Journal de Genève* (16,032) are the two best-known liberal papers in French-speaking Switzerland. Both insist on their independence from the Liberal Party and it is for this reason that they are also read by people who are not Liberal supporters. The regular readership of these papers is considerably greater than the size of the vote given the party in elections.[15]

Today, the opinion press mainly restricts the expression of its political tone to editorials and commentaries. Although a newspaper may have the label of a political party, it may have no direct affiliation with that party and does not necessarily support it in elections. Often the subscribers of the daily opinion papers are not partisans of the political parties whose views may be presented in editorials.[16] These papers are appreciated for their serious approach and their high standards of reporting.

There are no papers in Switzerland which are published directly and alone by any of the various political parties. The papers are owned by private individual publishers, or by public or private companies. Some are run by cooperative printing enterprises, as in the case of the Social-Democratic or Communist papers.[17]

The Roman Catholic press, which is largely based in Central Switzerland, is in second place for the greatest number of papers. Most of the Catholic papers, however, have low circulations—e.g., the St. Gallen *Die Ostschweiz* (26,594), Fribourg's *La Liberté* (25,459), and *Le Nouvelliste et Feuille d'Avis du Valais* from Sion in the canton of Valais (30,509). Only the Lucerne *Vaterland* has a circulation rate exceeding 50,000. The Catholic vote in these areas, however, is generally much higher than would be suggested by the low circulation rates mentioned here.

Socialist papers also have small sales records, although the Social-Democratic Party in Switzerland usually has many supporters in elections. The socialist press has its largest readership in the German-speaking area, where its most important daily is Bern's *Tagwacht* (18,189 subscribers for approximately 60,000 votes). *Le Peuple—La Sentinelle* (circulation around 9,000) is the only socialist paper in French Switzerland, although the Social-Democratic Party usually finds strong support here. The reason for the low circulation of these papers is that the blue- and white-collar workers in Switzerland who belong to the Left are obliged to subscribe to union publications and therefore do not bother with the party-affiliated papers.[18]

This tendency is also true in the countryside where the Peasant, Artisan, and Bourgeois Party often mobilizes a substantial vote; papers affiliated with this political party habitually have low circulations.

The Geneva *Voix Ouvrière*, which sells in the vicinity of 8,000 copies, is the only communist daily in Switzerland. The Basel-based *Vorwärts*, a communist weekly, changed from its daily schedule several years ago because of financial difficulties.

The canton of Ticino's largest political paper, the *Giornale del*

Popolo (17,719), has a Catholic perspective. Other opinion papers in the area include: *Il Dovere* (12,851), a radical paper; *Popolo e Liberta* (7,143), conservative; and the *Libera Stampa* (5,165), socialist.

Changes in the Press

Despite the existence of these politically oriented papers in all parts of the country, the neutral or independent press (papers with no loose or strong ties to political parties) can boast the largest circulation figures and is by far the most rapidly growing press. This trend is causing radical changes to take place in the structure of the Swiss press. These changes are representative of those occurring in the ideology and dogma in Swiss life, whether in the political, the economic, or the social sphere. Importation of foreign periodicals, television programs, films, and popular music help to standardize the public taste. For example, West Germany's *Jasmin*, comparable to *Cosmopolitan*, is one of the top three in the Swiss-German magazine market. Only months after its appearance in Switzerland, it was selling 100,000 copies in a market of only 3.8 million German-speaking Swiss.[19] *Stern* and *Quick*, two German illustrated journals, have also gained popularity in Switzerland in the last decade and reach approximately 10 percent of the readers in the German section of the country. Two French magazines, the popular *Paris-Match* and *Jours de France*, both have high sales records in *la Suisse romande.*[20]

Penetration of Italian periodicals in the canton of Ticino is also considerable. In particular, *Epoca*, *Oggi*, and *Tempo* sell well in proportion to the number of Italian-speaking Swiss who live in this area.

The Swiss illustrated weeklies are suffering because of the interest in foreign publications shown by the Swiss. Although the Swiss magazine market is not in a state of rapid decline, it is definitely stagnating. Swiss-German publications particularly are affected by the foreign competitors. *Schweizer Illustrierte Zeitung*, for example, had 221,644 readers in 1954 and 212,102 in 1970.[21]

Migration has resulted from continuous industrialization. Many people now move from place to place, with the result that the community sentiment as it was known in the past is dwindling. This has a direct correlation with interest in the local press. Because new or comparatively new residents of local communities are seldom greatly interested in local events, many Swiss have been turning to the big dailies, which give good coverage of national and international events.

The rising educational level also has distinct implications for the press: many readers today are turning to papers with large editorial resources. The new generation of readers is generally more sophisticated and wants the press to present news and offer background but to avoid opinion. A great many Swiss are politically independent and make up their mind on every issue. Many, in fact, change their attitudes from one issue to another. If a newspaper has the tab of a political party, it is bound to remain very limited in its circulation and influence.[22] The big super-regional papers are experiencing a tremendous increase in circulation, while growth of the opinion press has been stunted. The propensity is toward more information and less opinion. Table IV shows that the independent press has the majority of the large circulation dailies.

TABLE IV
DAILIES WITH CIRCULATIONS OF 50,000 AND OVER
(Political Orientation)

Name of Paper	Place of Publication	Circulation	Political Orientation
Blick	Zurich	239,058	Independent
Tages-Anzeiger	Zurich	218,201	Independent
Neue Zürcher Zeitung	Zurich	92,116	Radical
Feuille d'Avis de Lausanne	Lausanne	90,105	Independent
National-Zeitung	Basle	80,463	Radical
La Suisse	Geneva	67,371	Independent
Tribune de Genève	Geneva	62,917	Independent
Tribune de Lausanne	Lausanne	61,361	Independent
Luzerner Neueste Nachrichten	Lucerne	56,106	Independent
Berner Tagblatt	Bern	55,679	Independent
Der Bund	Bern	51,656	Radical
Vaterland	Lucerne	51,554	Catholic

Source: **Catalogue de la presse Suisse**, 1972.

CHANGES IN THE PRESS

Newspaper publishers are becoming aware of these new trends and have been particularly influenced by the unexpected success of Switzerland's first popular daily, the Zurich-based *Blick*. This paper, launched in 1959, began with a circulation rate of 48,000 copies. Its "sex and crime" formula made it an instant success and it now has the highest circulation rate in the country—267,499 in 1972. Its modern editorial methods and lavish use of pictures indicate a sharp contrast to the conservative style of the majority of newspapers in German Switzerland.[23]

From the start, *Blick* attempted to seek a national readership. Unlike all other Swiss papers it does not cater to a particular region or locality and includes no special local news pages. It has readers in all sections of the country but particularly in German Switzerland (see Table V). In the past few years, *Blick* has had its greatest gains in the rural areas of Switzerland rather than in the cities. The penetration of this paper into the countryside will upset the local press in these sections of the Confederation.

In 1967 another popular daily was begun under the name of *Neue Presse*. This paper was the cooperative production of the well-established *Tages-Anzeiger* and the *National-Zeitung*. *Neue Presse* attempted to be more informative than *Blick*, particularly in the political and economic fields. It was designed to take advantage of the lack of mid-day papers and to reach readers in urban centers who wanted quick news on the latest developments of the day. In 1968, however, it was forced to move its press time to the morning in order to extend its sales period. In 1969, it ceased publication altogether, suffering from problems arising out of a well-saturated market. The overriding cause for *Neue Presse*'s demise was that the owners belatedly realized that the paper would achieve break-even circulation only if its level were lowered below the point they were prepared to tolerate.[24]

There have been no further attempts to develop a paper like *Blick* in Switzerland. Plans to publish a French popular daily in *la Suisse romande* in 1965, under the name *Tribune Romande*, did not materialize. It is believed that the semi-popular dailies like *La Suisse* and *Tribune de Lausanne* have saturated the market and leave little room for a new popular daily.[25] In addition, the investment necessary to organize a paper of this kind would be prohibitive.

Although no popular papers have appeared on the Swiss press scene, there has been a general tendency to adopt some of *Blick*'s

TABLE V

BLICK'S SALES DISTRIBUTION 1970*

Cantons	Sales
Zurich	54,704
Bern	37,803
Basle	24,280
Aarau	18,342
St. Gallen	14,343
Soleure	11,651
Lucerne	9,071
Grisons	6,453
Thurgovie	5,614
Ticino	2,643
Valais	2,617
Fribourg	2,354
Vaud	2,300
Geneva	2,098
Neuchâtel	933

*In number of copies

LANGUAGE DISTRIBUTION OF BLICK

Language	Sales
German (Eastern and Northern Switzerland)	196,354
French (Western Switzerland)	10,302
Italian (Canton of Ticino)	2,643

Source: **Fichier de la Presse Suisse, 1971** (Swiss Press Archives).
(Latest distribution figures available.)

characteristics to existing papers. Publishers of general information papers have examined their format for changes and many have attempted to modify their typographical method, avoiding the austere appearance of the past. Some newspapers (e.g., *La Tribune de Genève* and *La Tribune de Lausanne*) have undergone a restyling to meet the readers' tastes for simple lines and pure forms.[26]

General information papers are now including human interest stories more frequently and the editorial language has been simplified. There is a trend toward personalization of information.

That the younger reader is being considered is seen in the introduction of special youth-oriented features in supplementary pages. Opinion papers are also watching trends in order to meet the changing taste of their readers. Mr. Bernard Béguin, former editor in chief of the *Journal de Genève* states that "the new generation of readers require more interpretation and less opinion. They care little about the opinion of the editorial staff but they are still interested in an explanation. The subscribers of the older generation would still like the paper to say 'this is good' or 'this is bad,' but the newer generation, particularly the students, would simply like to have a good background on situations."[27] Editorials of the opinion press still discuss referendum issues, but they are careful to allow the voter to make up his own mind on the issue.

The advent of the popular press and the move toward modernization of existing papers has stirred up factions in the press on both sides: some editors and publishers look forward to an updating of the press; others worry about the implications of a change in the press structure. Those who advocate change in the press and a restyling in both outlook and the appearance of the press maintain that presently many papers are provincial in tone and lack quality journalism. They claim that the overabundance of newspapers in Switzerland is the prime reason for the existence of numerous papers that are poorly edited and low in resources. Mr. Peter Uebersax, former editor of *Neue Presse*, states that "the vast majority of papers have so few on the editorial staff that the editor and his assistants, apart from any possible political engagement, have to limit themselves to preparing agency messages and reports of a few part-time local correspondents for the printer and to writing leading articles."[28]

On the other side, some editors and publishers feel that a structural change in the Swiss press will have a serious effect on the country's political life. Opponents of concentration fear that local individualism will be diminished as newspapers reach a regional audience rather than a local one. They also argue that direct democracy has been conditioned by the decentralized press and that diversity in the press is the key to the success of this political system. With the growth of the new press they foresee a loss of the educational function of newspapers and a general decline in quality.[29]

Trends Foreseen in the Near Future

In any case, there is no doubt that structural changes are taking place in the Swiss press. The trend toward press concentration takes many forms—editorial and technical concentration and concentration in advertising and of newspaper offices. This structural change of the Swiss press will have far-reaching implications for most newspapers. The quality dailies will experience the greatest growth while opinion papers will show circulation declines. The popular press is expected to cease its rapid growth rate of the past and may meet competition from the mass media.[30] The "in between" papers, those that try to be both local and general information papers, are in the greatest danger of extinction. However, there will still be room for well-edited local papers.

Cooperation exists in a variety of forms. The "Kopfblätter" is beginning to emerge on the press scene and may become popular in the near future. In this kind of arrangement, local editions of newspapers are prepared elsewhere, each having the same general news but containing different local news items and having their own *Kopf* or masthead.[31] Another method, suggested by Mr. Josef Jäger, attempts to limit the consolidation of local papers by the formation of a cooperative network. A central editorial staff would be appointed by a number of non-competitive papers sharing the same political and denominational views. This staff would supply member papers with news from home and abroad through a TTS network. A cooperative enterprise like this would allow editors to spend more time on the preparation of local news items, and would prevent the merger of local papers with larger papers.[32] A lack of cooperation among the local press, however, may result in its becoming a weekly press.

The opinion press may have to be satisfied with regional consolidation, since readers are turning away from ideological journalism. One paper alone representing a particular political viewpoint may be sufficient for each of the four language areas.[33] The popular press and mass media will continue to bring about changes in the style of the press. In addition, information will become more personalized and the traditional abstract treatment will be diminished. A national press is almost impossible to envision due to the cultural and linguistic differences in the country, but a regional press will predominate over the present local system. This will inevitably cause greater uniformity, but the consolidation of editorial resources should enable papers to provide better reporting in every field.

Advertising, the main source of income for the written press, will turn almost exclusively to the large circulation dailies with growth potential. Medium-sized and small papers, which have a more diversified distribution, will lose advertisers. "Give-aways" or *Anzeiger* (advertising sheets) are growing in number and are a real threat to the smaller papers.

Television advertising, which was introduced in 1965, was thought to have a serious influence on the volume of press advertising. Many newspapers did lose some of their brand goods advertising during 1965, but some advertisers returned to their press advertising a year later. This may have been due to the restrictions on television advertising (e.g., advertising is broadcast only at night between 7:00 and 8:30). In addition, certain kinds of advertising are barred from television (such as political or religious propaganda), and advertising of certain products is also restricted (medical products, alcohol, and tobacco).[34]

The introduction of radio advertising is expected by 1974, but it may appear before that time due to the influence of certain pressure groups.[35] The volume of press advertising, particularly in low circulation papers, will be affected.

Switzerland's decentralized, diversified press stands out as a unique situation at a time when countries have already been through the concentration of press enterprises. Although cantonal borders will be broken down due to social mobility and the further development of industrial centers, linguistic and cultural boundaries will help to maintain a certain degree of diversity in the Swiss press.

FOOTNOTES

1. *Catalogue de la presse Suisse, 1972* (Zurich: Association d'Agences Suisses de Publicité AASP, 1972), p. 13.

2. Correspondence from Mr. Josef Jäger, director of Schweizerische Politische Korrespondenz, Bern.

3. Pierre Béguin, "The Press in Switzerland," *Gazette: International Journal for Mass Communication Studies*, No. 2, 1967, p. 95.

4. *Ibid.*, p. 96.

5. Correspondence from Mr. Franz Mächler, editor in chief of *Nebelspalter* Rorschach.

6. Correspondence from Dr. M. Ungerer, editor of *Schweizerische Handelszeitung*, Zurich.

7. *Catalogue de la presse Suisse, 1972*, p. 13.

8. Ernst Bollinger, "Structural Picture of the Swiss Press: Trends and Prospects," *Gazette: International Journal for Mass Communication Studies*, No. 3, 1970, p. 155.

9. United Press International Office, Zurich.

10. André Siegfried, *Switzerland: A Democratic Way of Life* (Neuchâtel: La Baconnière, 1950), p. 131. The origin of the *Landsgemeinde* dates back to 1387 when the canton of Glarus held its first assembly of this type. There are five cantons that retain this tradition today: Glarus, Appenzell Outer Rhodes, Appenzell Inner Rhodes, Obwalden, and Nidwalden. Annually, on a Sunday in the spring, all enfranchised citizens in each of these cantons meet at some historic spot to elect their governors and make their laws.

11. *Ibid.*, p. 145.

12. Correspondence from Mr. Josef Jäger.

13. Hans Huber, *How Switzerland Is Governed* (Zurich: Schweizer Spiegel Verlag, 1968), p. 32.

14. Andreas Thommen, "Population: 6,000,000, Languages: 4, Papers: 490," *IPI Report* (June 1967), p. 8.

15. These papers cannot be measured in importance by their circulation records. Both *Neue Zürcher Zeitung* and *Journal de Genève* have been included on the lists of "The World's Best Daily Papers" published by universities and other institutions.

16. Author's interview with Mr. J. Légeret, former editor of the Press Service of the Swiss Office for the Development of Trade, Lausanne.

FOOTNOTES

17. Thommen, "Population: 6,000,000," p. 8.

18. Béguin, "The Press in Switzerland," p. 99.

19. Correspondence from Mr. Peter Uebersax, former editor of *Neue Presse*, Zurich.

20. Basilio Riesco, "Press and Television Advertising in Switzerland," *Gazette: International Journal of Mass Communication Studies*, No. 2, 1967, p. 170.

21. Verband Schweizerischer Werbegesellschaften VSW, Zurich. (Latest figures available.)

22. Author's interview with Mr. Bernard Béguin, former editor in chief, *Journal de Genève*, Geneva.

23. Béguin, "The Press in Switzerland," p. 100.

24. Correspondence from Mr. Peter Uebersax.

25. Bollinger, "Structural Picture of the Swiss Press," p. 156.

26. Michel Couturier, "Restyling Page One . . . as a Show Case," *IPI Report* (July 1966), p. 6.

27. Author's interview with Mr. Bernard Béguin.

28. Peter Uebersax, "The Logical Step: Go National," *IPI Report* (November 1967), p. 8.

29. Peter Dürrenmatt, "Too High a Price for Economic Success," *IPI Report* (November 1967), p. 7. Also, *Wie Frei Ist die Presse?* (Bern, Hallwag, 1971), by the same author.

30. Bollinger, "Structural Picture of the Swiss Press," p. 168.

31. Theodor Gut, "Village Voices," *IPI Report* (June 1967), p. 10.

32. Josef Jäger, "Die Schweizerische Lokalpresse," *Gazette: International Journal for Mass Communication Studies*, No. 2, 1967, p. 191.

33. Bollinger, "Structural Picture of the Swiss Press," p. 168.

34. Riesco, "Press and Television Advertising in Switzerland," p. 171.

35. Correspondence from Mr. Jean-François Bruttin, secretary-general of the Swiss Center for Press Research and Promotion, Lausanne.

3

Swiss Book Publishing Prospects

Despite language barriers within the country and stiff competition from neighboring countries, the Swiss publishing industry has shown marked growth dating from World War II. This chapter will examine this development as well as the story of early printing and publishing in Switzerland.

Growth of Printing and Publishing

The history of Swiss printing begins in monasteries during the Middle Ages. In Carolingian times, manuscripts were handwritten in the monastery at St. Gallen, which was an important educational center. Switzerland's oldest known book was produced in the monastery at Beromünster in the year 1470, although the first book printed with moveable type was published in Basel in ca. 1468.[1] Basel became a flourishing center of learning after the founding of a university in 1460. During the latter part of the fifteenth century, Basel was the center of printing activity in Switzerland. Books and paper became major exports of the merchant city. Geneva was important during this time for the production of theological and popular books in French. In 1480, Zurich began some publishing activity although it was not until the sixteenth century that printing flourished in this city.

Basel, Geneva, and Zurich continued to be active in the printing sphere during the Reformation. In Basel, scholars, illustrators, and printers worked harmoniously to produce some of the finest examples of printed books of the period. Calvin and the numerous religious refugees from France had their effect on book publishing in Geneva during the early decades of the sixteenth century. Geneva served as the center of anti-Roman-Catholic publishing for France, the Netherlands, and Scotland. Several editions of the Bible were produced in Zurich during this era by followers of the Reformer Zwingli (Luther's Swiss counterpart).

Publishing in Romansch was at its highpoint during the Reformation. Several editions of the New Testament were printed in the canton of Grisons, often on presses set up by Italian Protestant refugees.

Printing saw a period of decline during the Counter-Reformation. The quality of the works produced suffered as interest in beautiful books waned. Religious restrictions caused additional problems for the printing trade. This dark period for printing in Switzerland was altered with the Age of Enlightenment at the beginning of the eighteenth century. Geneva benefited greatly from the aesthetic and intellectual ideas coming out of France. This was the age of Voltaire and Jean-Jacques Rousseau, the famous citizen of Geneva. Both of these literary giants had works published in Geneva.

One of the major achievements of eighteenth century publishing was the introduction of the encyclopedia. The "Société typographique" of Neuchâtel produced an encyclopedia in 19 quarto volumes entitled *Description des arts et métiers* from 1771 to 1783. This was modelled after the great *Encyclopédie* of Diderot and d'Alembert. Other encyclopedias were produced in Geneva.[2]

In Zurich, the famous publishing house Orell, Füssli, Gessner & Company edited the first German translations of Shakespeare, Swift, Thomson, and Butler. Professor J. J. Bodmer, a director of the firm, instigated the introduction of English literature into German literary culture in order to counteract the overwhelming French influence.[3]

Many intellectuals sought refuge in Geneva during the upheavals of the French Revolution. Madame de Staël was among the most prominent of this group. She surrounded herself with her literary friends at her château in Coppet on Lake Geneva. Some of her writings and those of Benjamin Constant, her close friend, were published in Geneva. The intellectual activity resulting from this new flood of French intellectuals served as an impetus to the printing trade.

After the turn of the century, the important publishing

activity was shifted back to Paris, which rapidly became the cultural center during the romantic era. Many Swiss-German authors took their manuscripts to the large firms in Leipzig which offered them wider possibilities than the small provincial firms in Switzerland. Thus, many of the well-known nineteenth century Swiss-German authors such as Gottfried Keller, Jeremias Gotthelf, Conrad F. Meyer, and Carl Spitteler had their major works published by German publishing houses.[4] Milan proved to be too strong a competitor to the Swiss-Italian publishing activity, which declined to a low ebb.

Swiss publishing centers lost their international reputation partially because of internal political problems which the country was experiencing. Much of Switzerland's creative force was involved in politics and the problems of creating the Swiss Federal State. The growth of industrialization became more important during this time, and advanced technology played a major role in the improvement of printing equipment and the mass production of books. Aesthetic taste in book design, however, did not keep pace with these technological advances. Book design was enlivened in the early 1900s because of new interest in graphic art by artists. The revival of book design in England and Germany also greatly influenced Swiss book designers. During the twentieth century, printing techniques were perfected and high-quality craftsmanship was shown in the trade. Today, Swiss publishing firms are extremely well equipped and maintain the tradition of high-quality craftsmanship for which the Swiss are well known.[5]

World War I provided a stimulus to the publishing enterprise in Switzerland. Many Swiss-German publishers, in particular, realized their responsibility to defend their moral values through the publication of books. As the Swiss publishing sphere became once more self-sufficient, the number of new publishers grew and book production increased. The book trade in Switzerland flourished as it had in the sixteenth and eighteenth centuries.

There was an even greater period of growth in the publishing industry during World War II. However, because books had to submit to certain restrictions in order to protect the principle of neutrality, a semi-military board of examiners was set up to deal with the censorship of books. This committee was immediately disbanded at the end of the war. This censorship did not prevent the Swiss book trade from reaching new levels during the war. This period became the "fateful hour" for Swiss publishing.[6]

TRENDS AND ACHIEVEMENTS

Swiss publishers were forced to go into new fields of publishing in order to provide books which had formerly been published in Germany. Before the war, Switzerland had depended on Germany to provide much of the technical and scientific literature. It was during this time that some publishing houses went into the field of medical publishing. In order to avoid infiltration from Nazi Germany, Switzerland's publishing firms also produced fiction and belles-lettres as well as school books and scientific works. The Swiss book trade was able to stay at this high level of growth after the war, despite the recovery of German publishing. Technical and scientific publishing continues to be an important field in the Swiss publishing industry today. Literary publishing, however, is still almost exclusively centered in Paris and Germany.

Trends and Achievements

The total number of books published annually has steadily increased in the last 25 years. In 1970, there was one book published per 974 persons. In proportion to the size of the German and French populations, Switzerland publishes much more than Germany or France.[7] Table VI gives a clear picture of the growth of book production in Switzerland after World War II.

In 1971, German books represented 61 percent of the total book production; French books, 27 percent; Italian books, 3 percent; and English books, 4 percent. Only 33 works were produced in Romansch.[8] Table VII shows the subject distribution.

The greatest number of titles appear in the literature category (15 percent); this is followed by science subjects (11 percent) and the social sciences (10 percent). Although the percentages may vary from year to year, the overall picture remains substantially the same.[9]

The main achievements in the post-war years were reached in the production of technical and scientific books of excellent quality. This field of publishing has benefited from the good name acquired by Swiss industry and engineering as well as by the technical schools and institutes whose reputation each year attracts a large number of foreign students.[10]

Quality art and picture books were also one of the major accomplishments of the post-war period. Publishers went into various types of specialty publishing in order to penetrate foreign markets. In

TABLE VI

BOOK PRODUCTION 1944—1971

Year	Titles
1944	3,831
1948	4,691
1950	3,527
1960	4,817
1961	4,747
1962	5,086
1963	4,931
1964	4,941
1965	5,202
1966	4,817
1967	5,270
1968	5,213
1969	6,028
1970	6,436
1971	6,087

Source: Bibliothèque Nationale Suisse, Annual Reports 1944-1971.

the art field, Editions d'Art Albert Skira, founded in 1928, stands out as one of the pioneers in quality color reproductions. Albert Skira began his venture into art publishing by buying illustrations from well-known artists such as Picasso and Matisse to illustrate his books. Skira stimulated a spirit of rivalry in technical perfection which gave Swiss publishing its reputation for quality throughout the world.

The 1930s saw the advent of the book club in Switzerland. Today, there are approximately 12 book clubs in the French- and German-speaking areas of the country, with a total membership of about 800,000.[11] Most members do not have membership with more than one club. It is estimated that the book clubs represent 25 percent of total book sales annually.[12] The number of books offered by the

TABLE VII

SUBJECT DISTRIBUTION 1971

Subject	Titles
Generalities	.85
Religion, Theology	417
Philosophy, Psychology	167
Law, Business	220
Economics, Statistics	243
Social Science	92
Political Science	79
Military Arts	14
Philology, Literary History	462
Belles-lettres	935
Juvenile Literature	344
Education	127
Scholarly Works (Theses)	121
Fine and Applied Art	304
Music Theater, Cinema	68
Music (Practical)	541
History, Folklore	481
Geography, Ethnography	182
Maps, Atlases	125
Medicine	276
Natural Science	206
Mathematics	46
Technology, Industry, Crafts	152
Commerce	64
Agriculture, Forestry, Home Economics	73
Sports	72
Miscellaneous	185
Talking Records	6
	6,087

Source: Bibliothèque Nationale Suisse, Annual Report 1971.

clubs is generally limited to 800. The subjects which predominate the book clubs' lists are juvenile literature, fiction, art, and general non-fiction. Some of the clubs also include records on their lists. The offers are often made through catalogs or book club magazines. Publishers believe that book clubs can be useful as a valuable second market and as a method of diminishing risks in the case of costly editions or new works. In 1956, the Swiss Booksellers' and Publishers' Association concluded an agreement with the most important Swiss book clubs to safeguard the interests of the retail book trade. The agreement, which was revised in 1969, dictates the manner in which publishing rights are granted with reference to the nature of presentation, date of publication, and to a certain extent the price difference.[13] In recent years particularly, book clubs have greatly contributed to the popularity of Swiss books and their reputation.

These achievements in Swiss publishing—technical and scientific works, art books, and book clubs—largely explain the very definite progress of exports in this field. In 1912 imports for books were valued at 18.5 million francs compared with 3.5 million worth of exports. Exports considerably exceeded imports in 1945: 25 million francs compared with 10 to 12 million.[14] Figures for 1971 show that exports for books (not including magazines or newspapers) again exceed imports: 187.5 million francs as opposed to 180.3 million. Thus, the export figure for books in 1971 surpasses that of one of Switzerland's traditional export products—chocolate.[15]

Table VIII gives a breakdown of imports and exports by country for the year 1971. These figures are only approximate since no distinction is made between the book exports of Swiss origin and those books which were merely printed in Switzerland on behalf of foreign firms. In addition, books produced abroad with Swiss imprints are not included in these figures.

France provides the leading market for Swiss publications, which is an indication of the contribution Swiss-French publishers make to Swiss publishing as a whole. Publishing in German, which is on a far larger scale, compares less favorably with competition from Germany and Austria. However, it is only natural that Switzerland purchases a large number of books from these two countries. This trend is followed in Italian-language publishing. Imports from Italy largely outrank the Swiss book export figures to that country, due to the number of Italians working in Switzerland. Book exports to English-

TABLE VIII

BOOKS: IMPORT AND EXPORT—1971
(in Swiss francs)

Country	Import	Export
Fed. Rep. of Germany	93,407,612	37,624,642
France	49,971,478	96,026,471
U.S.A.	5,269,646	15,624,924
Great Britain	4,454,015	6,559,691
Italy	12,880,653	4,731,466
Austria	4,462,015	3,741,569
Canada	112,071	3,056,780
Dem. Rep. of Germany	1,004,971	162,829
Belgium/Luxembourg	4,168,910	3,243,124
Netherlands	1,598,354	2,703,889
Sweden	678,521	2,086,600
Spain	248,703	704,950
Australia	17,735	2,160,038

Source: **Der Schweizer Buchhandel**, March 15, 1972, p. 198.

language countries have increased in recent years; the United States is now the third largest buyer of Swiss books.[16]

It is essential that Switzerland continue its progress in penetrating foreign markets since the Swiss market is relatively limited. Because the country is divided into four language groups, Swiss publishers do not even have the entire country as a possible market and as a rule reach only members of their own language group. For this reason, most publishers must rely on foreign sales of their books.

To date, systematic book research does not exist in Switzerland. Universities and institutions have not yet turned their attention to scientific research of the book trade, book production, or reading habits. One investigation of the book trade was made in 1959 by the Institute of Business Administration at St. Gallen. This study was undertaken to find ways of increasing productivity in the Swiss publishing industry and to ameliorate economic conditions of the retail book trade.[17] Apart from some theses on the subject, this study represents the only scientific work on publishing in Switzerland, but despite its aims, this research had little effect on the publishing situation.

The increase in book production after the war years brought about an improvement in book design. The German typographer Jan Tschichold, who came to Switzerland in 1933, did much to improve the state of Swiss typography. His own typographical work in various Swiss publishing firms served as a model to others in the field. He wrote several publications on the art of printing and influenced firms to renew and enlarge their stock of type faces as a result of his teaching. The fact that many firms today have a large selection of type faces both for machine (Linotype, Intertype, Monotype) and hand composition can be largely attributed to Tschichold's groundwork. Tschichold preferred "classical" typography, which is somewhat less in favor today than the more modern typography. Classical typography, however, is still used for literary and scholarly books, while illustrated works and technical publications usually employ "modern" typographic treatment.[18] Other typographers who contributed to the reawakening of book design in Switzerland are Imre Reiner, Hans Vollenweider, and Max Caflisch.[19]

In 1944, the Swiss Booksellers' and Publishers' Association initiated an award system for the best designed Swiss books, with the hope of upgrading standards. The jury is composed of one member from each of the following organizations: the Swiss Book Printers' Association, the Swiss Work Alliance, the Association of Swiss Book- binders, the Association of Swiss Illustrators, the Union of Swiss Typographers, and representatives of book trade associations. The judging consists of an examination of the subject, lay-out, printing, binding, and the dust-cover, plus the overall impression of each book. The categories of works judged include fiction, science, textbooks, art, photography, juvenile literature, and special limited editions. The winners are publicized in a pamphlet and in window displays of bookstores. These annual awards generally promote Swiss books and help to educate the reading public aesthetically.[20]

Thanks to her central position, Switzerland can often take advantage of joint publishing ventures. The co-production method is often applied to heavily illustrated multilingual works, such as art books. Co-production results in a rational use of the technical means placed at the disposal of publishers and at the same time fully satisfies printers.[21] Co-production may also be employed for the simultaneous publishing of a book in two languages. Swiss publishers sometimes collaborate with publishers in Great Britain, France, or Germany, in order to balance the risks of a high-priced book.

One way of compensating for the risks involved in publishing is the translation of books. Switzerland, with its many linguists, is in an ideal position to carry out this function. The publisher is able to gain new rights from the publication of translations and, in this way, he is often able to make an appreciable profit. For effective and accurate translation, it is vital that the translator work from another language into his mother tongue. Therefore, a Swiss-German publishing house may undertake the project of translating a book from French into German, but it would rarely attempt to translate a German work into French. Many publishers have agreements with firms in other parts of Switzerland to translate works they believe may be successful in other language areas.

Out of a total of 6,087 new publications in 1971, 902 books were translated from foreign languages.[22] Approximately 48 percent of these were belles-lettres.[23] This large number of translations reflects the influences of the various cultural areas in Switzerland on each other. Anglo-Saxon influence is particularly evident in the German-speaking area of Switzerland, and the greatest number of translations are from English into German. A rather small percentage of German literature is translated into French and Italian whereas a larger share of French books are translated into German. Table IX gives additional statistics.

Organization of the Book Trade

The majority of Swiss publishing firms are small business with a limited output of titles. Many firms own printing operations or bookstores which help subsidize the publishing activities of the company. Approximately 27 percent of Swiss publishing firms own retail bookstores.[24] Smaller companies generally specialize in one limited subject area in order to minimize staff size. Some publishing houses developed from printing operations and a number were established in the eighteenth century. There is no real publishing center in Switzerland. For the most part, firms are scattered throughout the

TABLE IX

TRANSLATION STATISTICS—1971
(Of Works published in Switzerland)

From \ Into	German	French	Italian	Romansch	Other Languages*	Total
German	—	71	10	9	7	97
English	460	91	—	—	—	551
French	108	—	2	3	4	117
Dutch	12	1	—	—	—	13
Italian	17	3	—	—	—	20
Russian	15	8	—	—	—	23
Swedish	8	—	—	—	—	8
Spanish	4	1	—	—	—	5

*mainly English

Source: Bibliothèque Nationale Suisse, Annual Report 1971.

country, although there is a higher portion of publishing houses in the large cities such as Zurich and Basel in the German-speaking area.

The number of employees gives an indication of the size of the publishing firms. Table X includes only members of the Swiss Booksellers' and Publishers' Association (Schweizerischer Buchhändler- und Verleger-Verein, or SBVV).

At present the Swiss Booksellers' and Publishers' Association has approximately 150 members and 103 non-voting members (these are usually printers with limited publishing activities). There are 102 Swiss-German publishers, 50 publishers from the French-speaking area, and one from the Italian-speaking part.[25] The SBVV helps to promote Swiss books abroad and provides a means of cooperation among Swiss publishers and booksellers. It is mainly concerned with Swiss-German publishing activities.

The other major publishing association is the Association of Booksellers and Publishers in French Switzerland (Société des Librairies

TABLE X

SIZE OF PUBLISHING FIRMS

Employees	Publishing firms
30-	2
20-29	1
17-19	5
13-16	9
8-12	10
6-7	12
4-5	15
2-3	35
1 employee and/or owner	59

Source: Swiss Booksellers' and Publishers' Association, Zurich.

et Editeurs de la Suisse romande). These organizations actively cooperate with each other. The official joint journal of the two associations is *Der Schweizer Buchhandel* (*La Librarie Suisse*), which is published twice a month. The French-language publishing association has basically the same aims as the SBVV. The Société represents the six major regional associations of Fribourg, Geneva, Neuchâtel, Valais, Vaud, and the French-speaking part of the canton of Bern.

In addition to these two official trade associations, there are also denominational organizations. These include the Association of Catholic Booksellers and Publishers in Switzerland (Vereinigung katholischer Buchhändler und Verleger der Schweiz) and the Association of Protestant Booksellers and Publishers in Switzerland (Verband Evangelischer Buchhändler und Verleger der Schweiz). They promote their interests from within the SBVV and through other cultural associations.[26]

Switzerland complies with international copyright regulations including those of the Bern Convention and succeeding copyright conventions. It was not until 1884, when the Federal Constitution was revised, that a federal copyright law protecting literature and art was established in Switzerland. The most recent Swiss copyright law was revised in 1955.[27] Some publishers are in favor of a new law legalizing the use of photocopies but at the same time allowing the publisher to obtain compensation.[28]

Distribution of Swiss books is largely in the hands of the Swiss Book Center in Olten. It was founded in 1882 as a cooperative. Its main goal is to provide its members with better purchasing arrangements. Today, the Swiss Book Center functions as a wholesale firm and provides an efficient exporting system. The membership is made up of 202 booksellers.[29] Publishers have not been allowed to obtain membership. The Center publishes the *Lagerkatalog des Schweizer Buchzentrums, Olten*, which is a frequently used trade bibliography. It includes only in-print titles and in 1970 listed 35,000 works.[30]

The publishing house Office du Livre S.A. in Fribourg also acts as an important wholesale firm. It represents approximately 50 French, 30 German, and 10 Swiss firms in Switzerland.[31] Office du Livre holds an almost complete range of their production and publishes a catalog of its stock annually. The firm also produces an annual catalog of French-language Swiss books entitled "Ouvrages suisses de langue française." In addition, it publishes a catalog of Swiss periodicals. As an exporter, Office du Livre strictly limits its distribution to Swiss books which the firm sells to over 1,300 booksellers all over the world. There are some 130 other specialized firms dealing with the wholesale function.[32] Some publishing houses act in limited terms as trade distributors for other firms.

The retail trade is the most important means of marketing books in Switzerland despite the growth of book clubs and some mail-order bookselling. The approximately 417 bookstores and 187 other resale outlets in 262 towns provide a rather dense network of places where books are sold.[33] Sales take place at railway stations, department stores, and stationery shops as well as at bookstores. Most specialty bookstores are found in large cities and are often located near universities. Fields such as religion, medicine, psychology, and geography predominate in the specialized bookshop business.

Most bookstores are small operations, often affiliated with printing firms or publishing houses. There are a limited number of chain-type businesses in bookselling, although some firms have been enlarging their operations in the last few years. The major portion of the retail book trade is centered in Zurich, Lausanne, Basel, and Bern.

There are no book fairs offering purchasing facilities to the

retail trade in Switzerland although publishers and booksellers partici-
pate in Swiss trade exhibitions such as the Basel Trade Fair. Local
publishers' associations often organize book exhibitions for the public
in order to stimulate sales during the holiday season. Children's books
are displayed annually in cooperation with the Swiss Alliance for Youth
Literature (Schweizerischer Bund für Jugendliteratur).

Other means of promoting and advertising Swiss books include
cooperative efforts made by some publishers. The Swiss Booksellers'
and Publishers' Association sends a book catalog to all German-speaking
families just before the holiday season in December. In the past, most
advertising initiatives were limited to posters, catalogs, pamphlets, and
exhibitions. Publishers are now making more and more use of the mass
media. Both radio and television devote a large share of time to the
discussion of literature and new publications. Book reviews published in
newspapers and literary journals or given on radio and television also
help to promote new books, although reviewers do not always report
on Swiss books. Children's books are frequently reviewed in teachers'
journals and other periodicals devoted to juvenile literature.

The State of Swiss Publishing

The Swiss book market can be reduced to three parts,
following the cultural regions of the country, with the result that Swiss
publishers must export the major portion of their books. Swiss
publishing is therefore characterized by its international scope. Swiss
firms have penetrated the international market largely by specializing.
It is essential that Swiss publishers produce books in areas where there
is an obtainable market. Some smaller firms confine themselves to very
limited fields such as numismatics, whereas a few larger firms have gone
into more competitive areas such as medicine. Superior quality in
graphic art and technical skills in book design have served as a positive
force in the specialty book field.

Mr. Peter Oprecht, head of the Swiss Booksellers' and
Publishers' Association, believes that specialty publishing is the greatest
strength of Swiss firms. It is the key to finding a market for their
books. Co-production and the sale of translation rights have also served
to improve the economic state of the publishing industry.

Paperbacks have proved to be a successful form of book
production in Switzerland. However, few Swiss firms have been able to

take advantage of this field because of their limited market. Paperback publishing has principally been left up to a few large, well-organized publishing houses with wider markets.

The production of primary school books in German-speaking Switzerland is for the most part handled by publishing firms which are directly supported by the cantons. In most French-speaking cantons, private firms are able to exploit this market, although a substantial number of educational publications are imported from France. University and secondary school textbook publishing has been a relatively lucrative business with Swiss publishers.

Literary publishing has suffered in recent years because of the emphasis on general non-fiction, technical, and scientific works. Consequently, in spite of the flourishing state of Swiss publishing, a Swiss writer has more difficulty in getting published than his predecessors did 25 or 50 years ago. The public shows little interest in their own native authors unless they are first acclaimed by Paris or Frankfurt. For this reason, and to seek wider exposure, many Swiss writers go abroad to have their works published.[34]

Numerous literary prizes are awarded annually but these have little influence on the public and usually involve only a small sum of money. These awards, which include the "Prix Charles Veillon," the "Prix de la Guilde du Livre," and the "Prix de l'Alliance culturelle romande," serve mainly to honor authors. Few Swiss authors are able to live by their writing. The exceptions include Max Frisch and Friedrich Dürrenmatt, who are the leading Swiss-German writers today. Both of these authors have most of their works published in Germany.

Pro Helvetia, the publicly funded foundation which serves to promote Swiss cultural life abroad, provides some financial assistance to aspiring authors. Every year, two or three grants are given to writers who have already shown considerable literary promise. These grants are awarded to German-, French-, and Italian-speaking Swiss authors on an equal basis.[35] The Romansch group is given special funds for the production of linguistic and literary works in the Romansch language. Since the language is of such limited interest, it must be artificially kept alive by aid of this kind. Pro Helvetia finds that it is difficult to find writers in the Romansch area who are willing or able to meet the qualifications of this monetary award.

Pro Helvetia also provides some financial assistance to publishing firms for the production of special issues relating to Swiss cultural life. The National Fund in Bern supplies annual subsidies of up to approximately one million francs for scientific works.[36]

There is virtually no direct financial support to the publishing industry from the federal government. This stems from the fact that cultural matters are strictly the affair of the cantons—not the federal government. At the present time, there are no export incentives for the book trade, although this is an area that is being explored by a federal committee studying Swiss cultural affairs.

Despite the small size of Swiss firms, there has not been a problem of foreign take-overs. In the event of a firm's being threatened by a possible foreign take-over, the Swiss Booksellers' and Publishers' Association would provide support and seek financial backing.[37] Concentration in the publishing realm has also been limited. Most publishers are content to keep small publishing operations in order to reduce costs and minimize risks. New publishers in the field generally have outside financial assistance and do not depend solely on their publishing enterprise.

At present, publishers are trying to find more ways of cooperating, especially to improve and seek benefits through advertising and distribution. Some publishers believe that if firms do not find new methods of cooperation, consolidation within the industry will be inevitable. A group of nine Swiss publishers called "Treffpunkt 9" have been successful in finding cooperative methods, mainly in advertising. Annually they produce a joint book catalog called "Bücherpick" which is available before Christmas. In 1971, it included almost 5,000 titles in 12 different subject categories.[38] The group meets regularly to discuss problems of the publishing industry. They are particularly interested in encouraging Swiss writers and allocate approximately 300,000 francs each year for the production of Swiss works.[39] Dr. Josef Rast, a spokesman for "Treffpunkt 9," believes that it is of vital importance for publishers to join cooperative efforts. He feels that "spiritual unions" of this kind are necessary in order to avoid concentration and the loss of individualism in publishing. Dr. Rast is of the opinion that more efforts are needed to advertise and promote Swiss books.

Swiss Publishing: A Model for Other Multilingual Nations

The Swiss publishing industry has substantially overcome its problems of language and outside competition to build an impressive record. In the five-year period from 1967 to 1971, Switzerland's book production climbed by 15 percent.[40] Book exports increased by 58 percent during the same period.[41] Specialty publishing, quality publications, and limited publishing programs largely explain the Swiss success. The financial backing some Swiss firms receive through associated enterprises (printing operations, bookstores) is also an important factor.

Canada's floundering publishing sphere might learn from the Swiss example. This country also has to deal with a bilingual society and seemingly impenetrable competition from the United States. Book publishing in Canada has been called an "act of lunacy,"[42] and the state of the industry has not radically improved despite considerable government assistance. Publishers point out that books from the United States and Great Britain swamp the Canadian market. In addition, Canadian book exports are meager. Some Canadian firms have been able to support themselves by acting as agents for American publishing houses, but this does not solve the problem.

The national consciousness that has been sweeping over Canada has crept into the book publishing industry. This is perhaps the vital difference between Canadian and Swiss publishing. There is barely anything typically Swiss about the book trade in Switzerland although books on national issues are continually published. A substantial portion of Canadian publishing, on the other hand, centers on Canadian problems and viewpoints. Fear of American domination is the major cause of this trend. Take-overs by American firms are a real threat. The federal government has been able to intervene in certain cases, and some firms have cut back their publishing programs in order to reduce costs. Cooperative efforts among publishers, along with financial backing through the acquisition of profit-making enterprises, may help to improve the situation.

The book trade in other multilingual countries such as Belgium and South Africa also has had to overcome language barriers and strong outside competition. The problem is always to find marketable books in order to penetrate foreign markets. Switzerland's success in this domain may serve as an example to the publishing industries in other polyglot nations.

Conclusion

Switzerland is a land of geographical contrasts, diverse cultures, and four languages, while the decentralized governmental structure serves as another indication of Switzerland's diversified nature.

This characteristic is maintained in the publishing sphere; both the press and the book trade industry have a varied structure. In recent years, however, the press has been experiencing radical changes toward concentration. Popular papers have the highest circulation rates, whereas the small, politically-oriented newspapers are losing ground. Changes of taste in society largely explain these developments.

The book publishing industry has been undergoing a period of growth dating from the post-World War II period. Most publishers depend on foreign book sales because of the limited and linguistically divided book market in Switzerland. New publishing developments and quality books have helped to spread the reputation of Swiss publications.

The heterogeneous society in Switzerland necessitates a diverse publishing realm both in the press and in book publishing. The various publishing domains exist side by side, following the linguistic contours of this multilingual nation.

FOOTNOTES

1. Willy Rotzler, "Book Printing in Switzerland," in *Book Typography 1815-1965, in Europe and the United States of America* (London, Ernest Benn Ltd., 1966), p. 287.

2. *Ibid.*, p. 295.

3. *Books of Switzerland, Catalogue of the British Council Exhibition of Swiss Books* (London: Suffolk Galleries, 1946), p. 18.

4. *Ibid.*, p. 19.

5. Rotzler, "Book Printing in Switzerland," p. 313.

6. *Ibid.*, p. 318.

7. Author's interview with Mr. Peter Oprecht, head of the Swiss Booksellers' and Publishers' Association, Zurich.

8. Bibliothèque Nationale Suisse, Annual Report 1971, p. 26.

9. *Ibid.*

10. Jean Hugli, "The Situation in Swiss Publishing," *Revue Industrielle et Commerciale*, 1966, p. 18.

11. Sigfred Taubert, ed., "Switzerland," in *The Book Trade of the World*, Vol. I (Hamburg: Verlag für Buchmarkt-Forschung, 1972), p. 449.

12. *Ibid.*

13. *Ibid.*

14. Rotzler, "Book Printing in Switzerland," p. 319.

15. *Der Schweizer Buchhandel* (March 15, 1972), p. 198.

16. *Ibid.*

17. Taubert, "Switzerland," p. 442.

18. Rotzler, "Book Printing in Switzerland," p. 320.

19. *Ibid.*

20. Taubert, "Switzerland," pp. 449-50.

21. H. Hauser, "The Future of Swiss Publishing," *Revue Industrielle et Commerciale*, 1966, p. 20.

22. Bibliothèque Nationale Suisse, Annual Report 1971, p. 27.

23. *Ibid.*, p. 25.

24. Taubert, "Switzerland," p. 452.

25. Author's interview with Mr. Peter Oprecht.

26. Taubert, "Switzerland," p. 439.

27. *Ibid.*, p. 445.

28. Correspondence from Dr. Christian Overstolz, Schwabe & Co. Verlag, Basel.

29. Taubert, "Switzerland," p. 451.

FOOTNOTES

30. *Ibid.*

31. Correspondence from Office du Livre S.A., Fribourg.

32. Taubert, "Switzerland," p. 452.

33. *Ibid.*

34. Correspondence from Mr. R. Junod, head of the Association of Booksellers and Publishers in French Switzerland.

35. Author's interview with Mr. Paul Adler, head of the Information and Press Service, Pro Helvetia, Zurich.

36. Author's interview with Mr. Paul Adler.

37. Author's interview with Mr. Peter Oprecht.

38. Josef Rast, "Gemeinsame Werbung—gross geschrieben," *Der Schweizer Buchhandel* (Jan. 1, 1971), p. 4.

39. *Ibid.*, p. 5.

40. Bibliothèque National Suisse, Annual Reports 1967-1971.

41. *Der Schweizer Buchhandel* (March 15, 1972), p.2,198.

42. Peter Martin, "An Act of Lunacy: Book Publishing in Canada," *The Canadian Banker* (March/April, 1971), p. 34.

4

Directory

Part A of the directory portion lists major newspapers by city. Cantonal abbreviations are noted next to the city name. Population statistics, which are for the year 1970, were obtained through the Federal Bureau of Statistics and the Swiss National Library in Bern. The sources of this compilation of newspapers are as follows:

Impressum, Schweiz. Handbuch für Redaktionaddressen. Zurich: Arbeitsgemeinschaft für Marktentwicklung, 1971.

Répertoire de la Presse Suisse. Geneva, Data Information Services, S.A., 1971/1972.

For further information the following publication is also helpful:

Editor and Publisher Yearbook. New York, Editors' and Publishers' Co., Inc., annual.

Part B, the listing of major publishing firms, was compiled almost entirely through answers to questionnaires. For further information, consult the *Adressbuch des Schweizer Buchhandels* (Zurich: Schweizerischer Buchhändler- und Verleger-Verein, 1971/72).

The following sources also provide up-to-date information on the book trade:

International Editions of *Publishers' Weekly*. New York: R. R. Bowker, annual. (Formerly *Publisher's World*.)

International Literary Market Place, European Edition. New York: R. R. Bowker, annual.

Internationales Verlagsadressbuch. München: Verlag Dokumentation (New York: R. R. Bowker). This directory has been revised several times since 1964.

Publishers' International Year Book. London: Alexander P. Wales, 5th ed., 1968.

Table XI provides a list of Swiss cantons and their abbreviations.

TABLE XI
CANTONS OF SWITZERLAND

Aargau	AG	Schaffhausen	SH
Appenzell	AR	Schwyz	SZ
Basel	BS, BL	Solothurn	SO
Bern	BE	Thurgau	TG
Fribourg	FR	Ticino	TI
Geneva	GE	Unterwald	NW, OW
Glarus	GL	Uri	UR
Grisons	GR	Valais	VS
Lucerne	LU	Vaud	VD
Neuchâtel	NE	Zug	ZG
St. Gallen	SG	Zurich	ZH

PART A: NEWSPAPERS

AARAU (AG)
Pop. 16,881

AARGAUER TAGBLATT
Bahnhofstrasse
5001 Aarau
Editor in chief: Dr. Kurt Lareida
Circulation: 26,909
Language: German

Telephone: (064) 22 63 34
Telex: Agat 68 146
Founded: 1846
Frequency: Daily except Sunday
Politics: Radical

A Z FREIER AARGAUER
Weihermattstrasse 94
5001 Aarau
Editor in chief: Mr. Silvio Bircher
Circulation: 11,922
Language: German

Telephone: (064) 22 24 85

Founded: 1905
Frequency: Daily except Sunday
Politics: Social Democrat

(This paper is a "Kopfblatter" of *AZ Ring Zurich*)

ALTSTATTEN (SG)
Pop. 9, 084

RHEINTALISCHE VOLKSZEITUNG
Luterbachweg 3
9450 Altstätten
Editor in chief: Mr. Eugen Rohner
Circulation: 5,106
Language: German

Telephone: (071) 75 12 91

Founded: 1854
Frequency: 5 times weekly
Politics: Conservative

BADEN (AG)
Pop. 14,115

AARGAUER VOLKSBLATT
Rütistrasse 3
5400 Baden
Circulation: 13,556
Language: German

Telephone: (056) 2 55 04
Telex: 57 261
Founded: 1911
Frequency: Daily except Sunday
Politics: Catholic Conservative

64

BADENER TAGBLATT

5401 Baden

Editor in chief: Dr. O. Wanner
Circulation: 24,288
Language: German

Telephone: (056) 2 68 88
Telex: tagbd ch 54 245
Founded: 1849
Frequency: Daily except Sunday
Politics: Neutral

BASEL (BS)
Pop. 212, 857

BASLER NACHRICHTEN

Dufourstrasse 40
4002 Basel
Director: Mr. Rudolf Suter
Circulation: 23,305
Language: German

Telephone: (061) 23 10 80
Telex: 62 149
Founded: 1845
Frequency: 11 times weekly
Politics: Liberal Democrat

BASLER VOLKSBLATT

Petersgasse 34
4001 Basel
Director: Dr. Eug. Fehr
Circulation: 16,961
Language: German

Telephone: (061) 25 81 66
Telex: basvo ch 62 604
Founded: 1873
Frequency: Daily except Sunday
Politics: Catholic

NATIONAL-ZEITUNG

St. Alban-Anlage 14
4002 Basel
Director: Mr. Heinrich Kuhn
Circulation: 80,463
Language: German

Telephone: (061) 22 50 50
Telex: nzbas ch 62 140
Founded: 1842
Frequency: Twice daily
Politics: Radical

BELLINZONA (TI)
Pop. 16, 979

IL DOVERE

Viale St. Franscini
6501 Bellinzona

Telephone: (092) 5 41 43
Telex: sasa ch 79 155

DIRECTORY

IL DOVERE (cont'd)

Editor in chief: Mr. Giuseppe Buffi
Circulation: 12,851
Language: Italian

Founded: 1875
Frequency: Daily except Sunday
Politics: Radical Liberal

POPOLO E LIBERTA

Piazza Governo
6501 Bellinzona

Telephone: (092) 5 12 45

Editor in chief: Mr. Attilio Grandi
Circulation: 7,143
Language: Italian

Founded: 1900
Frequency: Daily except Sunday
Politics: Conservative

BERNE (BE)
Pop. 162,405

BERNER TAGBLATT

Dammweg 9/Nordring
3000 Berne

Telephone: (031) 41 46 46

Editor in chief: Dr. R. Th. Weiss
Circulation: 55, 679
Language: German

Founded: 1888
Frequency: Daily
Politics: Independent

BERNER TAGWACHT

Giessereiweg 4
3007 Berne

Telephone: (031) 45 59 81

Editor in chief: Mr. Richard Müller
Circulation: 18,189
Language: German

Founded: 1894
Frequency: Daily except Sunday
Politics: Social Democrat

DER BUND

Effingerstrasse 1
3001 Berne

Telephone: (031) 25 12 11
Telex: 32 133

DER BUND (cont'd)

Editor in chief: Dr. Paul Schaffroth
Circulation: 51,656
Language: German

Founded: 1850
Frequency: 11 times weekly
Politics: Radical-Independent

NEUE BERNER ZEITUNG

Maulbeerstrasse 10
3001 Berne
Editor in chief: Mr. Anton Stadelmann
Circulation: 10,151
Language: German

Telephone: (031) 25 29 11
Telex: 32 175
Founded: 1919
Frequency: Daily
Politics: Bourgeois

BIEL/BIENNE (BE)
Pop. 64,333

BIELER TAGBLATT SEELANDER BOTE

2501 Biel

Editor in chief: Mr. F. Probst
Circulation: 27,285
Language: German

Telephone: (032) 2 42 71
Telex: 34 568
Founded: 1850
Frequency: Daily except Sunday
Politics: Independent

JOURNAL DU JURA/TRIBUNE JURASSIENNE

Freiestrasse 9-15
2501 Biel
Editor in chief: Mr. J.-P. Maurer
Circulation: 13,494
Language: French

Telephone: (032) 2 42 71

Founded: 1864
Frequency: Daily except Sunday
Politics: Neutral

DIRECTORY

BRUGG (AG)
Pop. 8,635

BRUGGER TAGBLATT
Effingerhof
5200 Brugg
Director: Dr. Hanspeter Widmer
Circulation: 4,338
Language: German

Telephone: (056) 41 40 50

Founded: 1900
Frequency: Daily except Sunday
Politics: Radical

BURGDORF (BE)
Pop. 15,888

BURGDORFER TAGBLATT
Friedeggstrasse 4
3400 Burgdorf
Director: Mr. Heinz Däpp
Circulation: 2,834
Language: German

Telephone: (034) 2 22 56

Founded: 1830
Frequency: 5 times weekly
Politics: Liberal

LA CHAUX-DE-FONDS (NE)
Pop. 42,347

L'IMPARTIAL
Rue Neuve 14
2300 La Chaux-de-Fonds
Editor in chief: Mr. Gil Baillod
Circulation: 30,780
Language: French

Telephone: (039) 21 11 35
Telex: 35 251
Founded: 1880
Frequency: Daily except Sunday
Politics: Neutral

CHUR (GR)
Pop. 31,193

BUNDNER TAGBLATT
Hartbergstrasse 7   Telephone: (081) 22 14 23
7000 Chur
Director: Mr. Adolf Oberhänsli   Founded: 1852
Circulation: 11,914   Frequency: Daily except Sunday
Language: German   Politics: Conservative

DER FREIE RATIER
Postfach   Telephone: (081) 22 15 31
7001 Chur
Editor in chief: Dr. D. Witzig   Founded: 1867
Circulation: 4,350   Frequency: Daily except Sunday
Language: German   Politics: Radical-Democrat

NEUE BUNDNER ZEITUNG
Kornplatz 6   Telephone: (081) 22 28 26
7000 Chur   Telex: 74 150
Editor in chief: Dr. Georg Casal   Founded: 1876
Circulation: 22,030   Frequency: Daily except Sunday
Language: German   Politics: Democrat-Independent

DELEMONT (BE)
Pop. 11,797

LE DEMOCRATE
Rue des Moulins 21   Telephone: (066) 2 17 51
2800 Delémont
Director: Mr. Jean Schnetz   Founded: 1877
Circulation: 11,408   Frequency: Daily except Sunday
Language: French   Politics: Radical Democrat

DIRECTORY

EINSIEDELN (SZ)
Pop. 10,020

SCHWYZER NACHRICHTEN
Postfach   Telephone: (055) 6 08 32
8840 Einsiedeln

Circulation: 2,712   Founded: 1946
Language: German   Frequency: Daily except Sunday
(This paper is a "Kopfblätter" of *Neuen Zürcher Nachrichten.*)   Politics: Catholic

FRAUENFELD (TG)
Pop. 17,576

THURGAUER VOLKSZEITUNG
Postfach   Telephone: (054) 7 18 45
8500 Frauenfeld

Circulation: 9,606   Founded: 1844
Language: German   Frequency: Daily except Sunday
(This paper is a "Kopfblätter" of *Neuen Zürcher Nachrichten.*)   Politics: Catholic

THURGAUER ZEITUNG
Postfach   Telephone: (054) 7 37 40
8500 Frauenfeld   Telex: 76 383
                                Founded: 1789
Circulation: 19,113   Frequency: Daily except Sunday
Language: German   Politics: Radical Democrat

FRIBOURG (FR)
Pop. 39,695

FREIBURGER NACHRICHTEN
Pérolles Strasse 40
1701 Fribourg
Editor in chief: Mr. Bruno Fasel
Circulation: 9,777
Language: German

Telephone: (037) 22 34 06
Telex: fnfr 36 100
Founded: 1863
Frequency: Daily except Sunday
Politics: Catholic Conservative

LA LIBERTE
Avenue de Pérolles 93
1700 Fribourg
Editor in chief: Mr. François Gross
Circulation: 25,459
Language: French

Telephone: (037) 22 26 22
Telex: 36 176
Founded: 1870
Frequency: Daily except Sunday
Politics: Catholic Conservative

GENEVA (GE)
Pop. 173,618

LE COURRIER
Rue du Vieux-Billard 1
1211 Geneva 4
Director: Mr. Jean-Pierre Chalier
Editor in chief: Mr. Roger Villard
Circulation: 16,208
Language: French

Telephone: (022) 24 32 45
Telex: 22 928

Founded: 1867
Frequency: Daily except Sunday
Politics: Catholic

JOURNAL DE GENEVE
Rue Général-Dufour 5/7
1211 Geneva 11
President: Mr. Raymond Deonna
Editor in chief: Mr. Claude Monnier

Telephone: (022) 25 03 50
Telex: 22 214 / 23 660

Founded: 1826

DIRECTORY

JOURNAL DE GENEVE (cont'd)

Circulation: 16,032
Language: French

Frequency: Daily except Sunday
Politics: Liberal

LA SUISSE

Rue des Savoises 15
1211 Geneva 11
Editor in chief: Mr. Marc Chenevière
Assistant editor: Mr. Claude Richoz
Circulation: 60,773
Language: French

Telephone: (022) 26 22 00
Telex: 27 666

Founded: 1898
Frequency: Daily
Politics: Independent

LA TRIBUNE DE GENEVE

Rue du Stand 42
1211 Geneva 11
Editor in chief: Mr. G.-H. Martin
Assistant editor: Mr. A. Roulet
Circulation: 62,917
Language: French

Telephone: (022) 25 82 80
Telex: 22 110 / 22 876

Founded: 1879
Frequency: Daily except Sunday
Politics: Independent

VOIX OUVRIERE

Pré-Jérome 6
1211 Geneva 4
Editor in chief: Mr. Armand Magnin
Circulation: 8,000
Language: French

Telephone: (022) 25 63 18

Founded: 1945
Frequency: Daily except Sunday
Politics: Communist

GLARUS (GL)
Pop. 8,189

GLARNER NACHRICHTEN

Zwinglistrasse 6
8750 Glarus

Telephone: (058) 51 9 21
Telex: 75 491

GLARNER NACHRICHTEN (cont'd)

Circulation: 10,253
Language: German

Founded: 1874
Frequency: Daily except Sunday
Politics: Bourgeois

HERISAU (AR)
Pop. 14,597

APPENZELLER ZEITUNG
Schläpfer & Co. AG
9100 Herisau
Editor in chief: Mr. Paul Müller
Circulation: 13,710
Language: German

Telephone: (071) 51 31 31
Telex: Appzeitung 77 147
Founded: 1828
Frequency: Daily except Sunday
Politics: Liberal

KREUZLINGEN (TG)
Pop. 15,760

THURGAUER VOLKSFREUND
8280 Kreuzlingen
Editor in chief: Mr. Hanspeter Rederlechner
Circulation: 5,804
Language: German

Telephone: (072) 8 23 55
Founded: 1882
Frequency: Daily except Sunday
Politics: Bourgeois

LANGENTHAL (BE)
Pop. 13,007

LANGENTHALER TAGBLATT
Bahnhofstrasse 37
4900 Langenthal

Telephone: (063) 2 18 04

LANGENTHALER TAGBLATT (cont'd)

President: Prof. Hans Schneeberger
Circulation: 3,625
Language: German

Founded: 1864
Frequency: Daily except Sunday
Politics: Bourgeois

LANGNAU (BE)
Pop. 8,950

EMMENTHALER-BLATT
Dorfstrasse
3550 Langnau
Editor in chief: Mr. Fritz Zopfi
Circulation: 43,203
Language: German

Telephone: (035) 2 19 14
Telex: 32 187
Founded: 1845
Frequency: Daily except Sunday
Politics: Neutral Bourgeois

LAUSANNE (VD)
Pop. 137,383

FEUILLE D'AVIS DE LAUSANNE
Avenue de la Gare 33
1003 Lausanne
Editor in chief: Mr. Pierre Corday
Circulation: 90,105
Language: French

Telephone: (021) 20 31 41
Telex: 24 782
Founded: 1762
Frequency: Daily except Sunday
Politics: Independent

GAZETTE DE LAUSANNE
Rue de la Vigie 3
1001 Lausanne
Director: Mr. Emanuel Gottraux
Editor in chief: Mr. François Landgraf
Circulation: 25,955 (including *La
Nouvelle Revue de Lausanne*)
Language: French

Telephone: (021) 20 61 61
Telex: 24 534

Founded: 1798
Frequency: Daily except Sunday
Politics: Liberal

PART A: NEWSPAPERS

LA NOUVELLE REVUE DE LAUSANNE

Avenue Ruchonnet 15
1000 Lausanne
Editor in chief: Mr. Michel Jaccard
Circulation: 25,955 (including *Gazette de Lausanne*)
Language: French

Telephone: (021) 20 13 71
Telex: 24 161
Founded: 1868
Frequency: Daily except Sunday
Politics: Radical

TRIBUNE DE LAUSANNE/LE MATIN

Case Postale 1077
1001 Lausanne
Editor in chief: Mr. Jean Dumur
Assistant editors: Mr. Max Syfrig and
Mr. René Langel
Circulation: 61,361
Language: French

Telephone: (021) 20 31 31
Telex: 24 762/763/764

Founded: 1862
Frequency: Daily
Politics: Independent

LIESTAL (BL)
Pop. 12,500

BASELLANDSCHAFTLICHE ZEITUNG

Schützenstrasse 6
4410 Liestal
Editor in chief: Dr. F. Lüdin
Circulation: 14,039
Language: German

Telephone: (061) 84 17 71
Telex: 63 243
Founded: 1832
Frequency: Daily except Sunday
Politics: Bourgeois Radical

LUCERNE (LU)
Pop. 69, 879

LUCERNER NEUESTE NACHRICHTEN

Zürichstrasse 3
6000 Lucerne

Telephone: (041) 22 11 06
Telex: 78 122

75

DIRECTORY

LUCERNER NEUESTE NACHRICHTEN (cont'd)

Editor in chief: Dr. Alois Anklin
Circulation: 56,106
Language: German

Founded: 1897
Frequency: Daily except Sunday
Politics: Independent

LUZERNER TAGBLATT

Baselstrasse 11/13
Postfach
6002 Lucerne
Editor in chief: Dr. Bruno Laube
Circulation: 23,615
Language: German

Telephone: (041) 24 22 33
Telex: 78 177

Founded: 1852
Frequency: Daily except Sunday
Politics: Radical Democrat

VATERLAND

Postfach
6002 Lucerne
Editor in chief: Dr. Othmar Hersche
Circulation: 51,554
Language: German

Telephone: (041) 36 44 44
Telex: 78 288
Founded: 1871
Frequency: Daily except Sunday
Politics: Catholic Conservative

LUGANO (TI)
Pop. 22,280

CORRIERE DEL TICINO

Corso Elvezia 33
6900 Lugano
Director: Dr. G. Locarnini
Editor in chief: Mr. V. Maestrini
Circulation: 17,800
Language: Italian

Telephone: (091) 3 24 71
Telex: colug 79 289

Founded: 1890
Frequency: Twice daily
Politics: Neutral

GAZZETTA TICINESE

Via Mercoli 8
6900 Lugano

Telephone: (091) 51 27 44

GAZZETTA TICINESE (cont'd)

Circulation: 1,725
Language: Italian

Founded: 1801
Frequency: Daily except Sunday
Politics: Liberal Democrat

GIORNALE DEL POPOLO

Via Massagno 17
6903 Lugano Massagno
Editor in chief: Mr. Alfredo Leber
Circulation: 17,719
Language: Italian

Telephone: (091) 3 22 71
Telex: popol ch 79 112
Founded: 1926
Frequency: Daily except Sunday
Politics: Catholic

LIBERA STAMPA

Via L. Canonica 3
Casella Postale 26
6901 Lugano
Editor in chief: Mr. Silvano Ballinari
Circulation: 5,165
Language: Italian

Telephone: (091) 51 65 55
Telex: 79 372

Founded: 1913
Frequency: Daily except Sunday
Politics: Socialist

MONTREUX (VD)
Pop. 20,421

JOURNAL DE MONTREUX

Avenue des Planches 22
1820 Montreux
Editor in chief: Mr. P.-A. Luginbühl
Circulation: 5,446
Language: French

Telephone: (021) 62 47 62

Founded: 1867
Frequency: Daily except Sunday
Politics: Neutral

DIRECTORY

MUNSINGEN (BE)
Pop. 8,350

TAGES-NACHRICHTEN
3110 Münsingen

Editor in chief: Mr. Herbert Fischer
Circulation: 40,801
Language: German

Telephone: (031) 92 22 11
Telex: 32 417
Founded: 1883
Frequency: Daily except Sunday
Politics: Independent

NEUCHATEL (NE)
Pop. 38,784

FEUILLE D'AVIS DE NEUCHATEL
Rue St. Maurice 4
2000 Neuchâtel
Director: Mr. R. Aeschelmann
Editor in chief: Mr. J. Hostettler
Circulation: 35,100
Language: French

Telephone: (038) 25 65 01
Telex: 35 181 / 35 182

Founded: 1738
Frequency: Daily except Sunday
Politics: Independent

OLTEN (SO)
Pop. 21,209

OLTNER TAGBLATT
Ziegelfeldstrasse 60
4600 Olten
Editor in chief: Mr. M. Schnetzer
Circulation: 8,052
Language: German

Telephone: (062) 32 41 41

Founded: 1878
Frequency: Daily except Sunday
Politics: Radical Democrat

PART A: NEWSPAPERS

SOLOTHURNER AZ

4600 Olten   Telephone: (062) 21 27 91
Editor in chief: Mr. Walter Kräuchi
Circulation: 7,939   Frequency: Daily except Sunday
Language: German   Politics: Social Democrat

PFAFFIKON (ZH)
Pop. 7,473

TAGBLATT DES BEZIRKES PFAFFIKON

8330 Pfaffikon   Telephone: (051) 97 51 11
Director: Mr. Samuel Galle   Founded: 1957
Circulation: 5,540   Frequency: Daily except Sunday
Language: German   Politics: Democrat

PORRENTRUY (BE)
Pop. 7,827

LE PAYS

2900 Porrentruy   Telephone: (066) 6 10 13
Editor in chief: Mr. Jean Wilhelm   Founded: 1873
Circulation: 5,540   Frequency: Daily except Sunday
Language: French   Politics: Catholic

ROMANSHORN (TG)
Pop. 8,329

SCHWEIZERISCHE BODENSEE-ZEITUNG

Alleestrasse 22   Telephone: (071) 63 31 32
8590 Romanshorn

SCHWEIZERISCHE BODENSEE-ZEITUNG (cont'd)

Circulation: 3,531
Language: German

Founded: 1849
Frequency: Daily except Sunday
Politics: Radical Democrat

RORSCHACH (SG)
Pop. 11,963

OSTSCHWEIZERISCHES TAGBLATT
Signalstrasse 8
9400 Rorschach

Telephone: (071) 41 43 46

Founded: 1845
Circulation: 7,010
Language: German

Frequency: Daily except Sunday
Politics: Radical Democrat
(This paper is a "Kopfblätter" of the *St. Galler Tagblatt*.)

RORSCHACHER ZEITUNG
Kirchstrasse 20
9400 Rorschach

Telephone: (071) 41 22 88

Founded: 1899
Circulation: 3,788
Language: German

Frequency: Daily except Sunday
Politics: Catholic

ST. GALLEN (SG)
Pop. 80,852

DIE OSTSCHWEIZ
Hint. Poststrasse 2
9001 St. Gallen
Editor in chief: Dr. Hermann Bauer
Circulation: 26,594
Language: German

Telephone: (071) 22 23 34
Telex: 77 393
Founded: 1874
Frequency: Twice daily
Politics: Catholic

PART A: NEWSPAPERS

ST. GALLER TAGBLATT
Fürstenlandstrasse 122
9001 St. Gallen
Editor in chief: Mr. Hans Zollikofer, Jr.
Circulation: 45,577
Language: German

Telephone: (071) 27 42 42
Telex: 77 537
Founded: 1838
Frequency: Daily except Sunday
Politics: Radical Democrat

SCHAFFHAUSEN (SH)
Pop. 37,035

ARBEITER ZEITUNG (Schaffhauser AZ)
Webergasse 39
8200 Schaffhausen
Editor in chief: Mr. Hugo Leu
Circulation: 5,236
Language: German

Telephone: (053) 5 11 86

Founded: 1918
Frequency: Daily except Sunday
Politics: Social Democrat

(This paper is a "Kopfblätter" of *A Z Ring Zurich.*)

SCHAFFHAUSER NACHRICHTEN
Vordergasse 58
8200 Schaffhausen
Editor in chief: Dr. Carl Oechslin
Circulation: 20,222
Language: German

Telephone: (053) 4 23 21
Telex: 76 483
Founded: 1862
Frequency: Daily except Sunday
Politics: Bourgeois

SION (VS)
Pop. 21,925

NOUVELLISTE ET FEUILLE D'AVIS DU VALAIS
Rue de l'Industrie 13
1951 Sion
Editor in chief: Mr. André Luisier

Telephone: (027) 2 31 51/52

NOUVELLISTE ET FEUILLE D'AVIS DU VALAIS (cont'd)

Circulation: 30,509
Language: French

Frequency: Daily except Sunday
Politics: Conservative

SOLOTHURN (SO)
Pop. 17,708

SOLOTHURNER NACHRICHTEN
Werkhofstrasse 5
4500 Solothurn
Editor in chief: Dr. Josef Ziegler
Circulation: 12,816
Language: German

Telephone: (065) 2 32 67

Founded: 1961
Frequency: Daily except Sunday
Politics: Catholic Conservative

SOLOTHURNER ZEITUNG
Dornacherstrasse 35/39
4500 Solothurn
Editor in chief: Dr. Ulrich Luder
Circulation: 35,211
Language: German

Telephone: (065) 2 64 61
Telex: vssz ch 34 204
Founded: 1907
Frequency: Daily except Sunday
Politics: Radical Democrat

SPIEZ (BE)
Pop. 9,911

BERNER OBERLANDER
Seestrasse 42
3700 Spiez
Editor in chief: Mr. Ernst Maurer
Circulation: 14,207
Language: German

Telephone: (033) 54 44 44

Founded: 1898
Frequency: Daily except Sunday
Politics: Bourgeois

PART A: NEWSPAPERS

STAFA (ZH)
Pop. 9,937

ZURICHSEE-ZEITUNG
Seestrasse
8712 Stäfa
Editor in chief: Dr. Theodor Gut
Circulation: 18,207
Language: German

Telephone: (01) 73 81 01

Founded: 1845
Frequency: Daily except Sunday
Politics: Bourgeois

THUN (BE)
Pop. 36,523

THUNER TAGBLATT
Rampenstrasse 1
Postfach
3600 Thun
Editor in chief: Mr. Heinrich Kunz
Circulation: 11,133
Language: German

Telephone: (033) 3 30 31

Founded: 1876
Frequency: Daily except Sunday
Politics: Bourgeois

VEVEY (VD)
Pop. 17,957

FEUILLE D'AVIS DE VEVEY
Rue du Lac 49
1800 Vevey
Editor in chief: Mr. Arnold Gétaz
Circulation: 8,138
Language: French

Telephone: (021) 51 21 56
Telex: fav ch 24 924
Founded: 1846
Frequency: Daily except Sunday
Politics: Neutral

DIRECTORY

WETZIKON (ZH)
Pop. 13,469

DER ZURCHER OBERLANDER
8620 Wetzikon
Editor in chief: Dr. Karl Eckinger
Circulation: 16,139
Language: German

Telephone: (051) 77 25 56
Founded: 1961
Frequency: Daily except Sunday
Politics: Radical Democrat

WIL (SG)
Pop. 14,646

NEUES WILER TAGBLATT
9500 Wil
Editor in chief: Mr. A. Stadelmann
Circulation: 3,654
Language: German

Telephone: (054) 7 18 45
Founded: 1871
Frequency: Daily except Sunday
Politics: Catholic

WINTERTHUR (ZH)
Pop. 92, 722

DER LANDBOTE
Postfach 154
8041 Winterthur
Editor in chief: Dr. Arthur Baur
Circulation: 27,908
Language: German

Telephone: (052) 22 60 31
Telex: 76 441
Founded: 1836
Frequency: Daily except Sunday
Politics: Democrat

WEINLANDER TAGBLATT
Wülflingerstrasse 235
8408 Winterthur

Telephone: (052) 25 18 69

WEINLANDER TAGBLATT (cont'd)

Circulation: 5,020
Language: German

Frequency: Daily except Sunday
Politics: Neutral

WINTERTHURER ARBEITER-ZEITUNG (A Z)

Technikumstrasse 90
Postfach
8400 Winterthur
Editor in chief: Mr. Martel Gerteis
Circulation: 4,035
Language: German

Telephone: (052) 22 61 21
Telex: 76 493

Founded: 1897
Frequency: Daily except Sunday
Politics: Socialist

YVERDON (VD)
Pop. 20,538

JOURNAL D'YVERDON

Avenue Haldimand 6
1400 Yverdon
Editor in chief: Mr. François Perret
Circulation: 6,873
Language: French

Telephone: (024) 2 16 45
Telex: 24 725
Founded: 1773
Frequency: Daily except Sunday
Politics: Neutral

ZOFINGEN (AG)
Pop. 9,292

ZOFINGER TAGBLATT

4800 Zofingen
Editor in chief: Mr. Oskar Hedinger
Circulation: 12,962
Language: German

Telephone: (062) 51 17 34
Founded: 1872
Frequency: Daily except Sunday
Politics: Radical Democrat

ZUG (ZG)
Pop. 22, 972

ZUGER-TAGBLATT
Gubelstrasse 19
6301 Zug
Editor in chief: Mr. Richard Ammann
Circulation: 4,033
Language: German
(This paper is a "Kopfblätter" of *Luzerner Tagblatt*.)

Telephone: (042) 21 40 54
Telex: 78 731

Frequency: Daily except Sunday
Politics: Liberal

ZURICH (ZH)
Pop. 422, 640

BLICK
Staffelstrasse 8
8045 Zurich
Director and ed. in chief: Mr. Martin Speich
Circulation: 239,058
Language: German

Telephone: (01) 36 36 36
Telex: 55 388
Founded: 1959
Frequency: Daily
Politics: Independent

NEUE ZURCHER NACHRICHTEN
Holbeinstrasse 26
8008 Zurich

Circulation: 18,334
Language: German

Telephone: (01) 34 17 07
Telex: 53 661
Founded: 1895
Frequency: Daily except Sunday
Politics: Catholic

NEUE ZURCHER ZEITUNG
Falkenstrasse 11
8021 Zurich
Editor in chief: Mr. Fred Luchsinger
Circulation: 92,116
Language: German

Telephone: (01) 32 71 00
Telex: 52 157 / 158
Founded: 1779
Frequency: Twice daily
Politics: Radical

PART A: NEWSPAPERS

TAGBLATT DER STADT ZURICH
Postfach
8022 Zurich
Editor in chief: Mr. Ryk Huber
Circulation: 104,916
Language: German

Telephone: (01) 32 70 60

Frequency: Daily except Sunday
Politics: Independent

TAGES-ANZEIGER
Werdstrasse 21
8004 Zurich
Editor in chief: Mr. Walter Stutzer
Circulation: 218,201
Language: German

Telephone: (01) 39 50 50
Telex: 54 163
Founded: 1893
Frequency: Daily except Sunday
Politics: Independent

DIE TAT
Postfach
8023 Zurich
Editor in chief: Dr. Walter Biel
Circulation: 33,911
Language: German

Telephone: (01) 42 22 00
Telex: 52 166
Founded: 1935
Frequency: Daily except Sunday
Politics: Independent

ZURCHER AZ
Stauffacherstrasse 5
8021 Zurich
Editor in chief: Mr. Helmut Hubacher
Circulation: 16,113
Language: German

Telephone: (01) 39 33 00
Telex: 54 572

Frequency: Daily except Sunday
Politics: Socialist

PART B: PUBLISHING FIRMS

ABC VERLAG
    Stauffacherquai 40   Telephone: (01) 23 16 73
    8021 Zurich   Founded: 1931
Chairman of the Board: Mr. K. Baumann
Assistant Director: Mr. E. Baumgartner
Production Manager: Mr. Wagner
Titles published, 1971: 6   Titles in stock: 25
Subjects of books published: art, business, medicine, psychology
Languages of publications: German, French, English (in multilingual texts)

DIE ARCHE VERLAG AG
    Rosenbühlstrasse 37   Telephone: (01) 34 21 54
    8044 Zurich   Cable: Archeverlag
Managing Director: Mr. Peter Schifferli   Founded: 1943
Titles published, 1972: 40   Titles in stock: 650
Subjects of books published: fiction, belles-lettres, politics, religion
Books distributed by: Verlag der Arche, Erikastrasse 11, 8003 Zurich.
Language of publications: German

ARTEMIS PUBLISHING CO., LTD.
(Artemis Publishers and Architectural Publications)
    Limmatquai 18   Telephone: (01) 34 11 00
    8024 Zurich   Founded: 1943
Chairman of the Board: Mr. Dieter Bührle
Managing Director: Mr. Bruno Mariacher
Assistant Director: Ms. Lydia Lehmann
Editor in Chief: Mr. Martin Müller
Rights and Permissions: Ms. Ingrid Parge
Production Manager: Mr. Walter Glättli
Art Director: Mr. Peter Rüfenacht
Titles published, 1972: 30   Titles in stock: 522
Subjects of books published: juvenile literature, architecture, classics,
    Swiss literature, picture books
Languages of publications: German, French, English

PART B: PUBLISHING FIRMS

ATLANTIS VERLAG
Zürichbergstrasse 66
8044 Zurich
Chairman of the Board: Dr. Max Mittler
Assistant Director: Dr. Daniel Bodmer
Titles published, 1973: 25

Telephone: (01) 32 53 43 / 32 54 97
Cable: Atlantisverlag
Founded: 1930

Titles in stock: 300
Subjects of books published: fiction, belles-lettres, music, juvenile literature
Languages of publications: German, English

ATRIUM VERLAG AG
Hofackerstrasse 36
8032 Zurich
Chairman of the Board: Mr. K. L. Maschler
Editor in chief: Mr. K. L. Maschler
Titles published, 1971: 2

Telephone: (01) 53 80 45
Founded: 1936

Titles in stock: 73
Subject of books published: juvenile literature
Language of publications: German
Foreign offices: Atrium Press Limited, 115 Gloucester Place, London W1
    (Tel. (01) 935 7151; Cable Famart London W1).

AUGUSTIN-VERLAG
8240 Thayngen
Owner: Mr. Karl Augustin
Managing Director: Mr. K. Augustin, Jr.
Assistant Director: Mr. Arnet
Titles published, 1971: 3

Telephone: (053) 6 71 31
Founded: 1911

Subjects of books published: anatomy (school books)
Language of publications: German
Periodicals: *Nature and Man*, bimonthly

BASILIUS-PRESSE AG
Güterstrasse 86
4002 Basel
Chairman of the Board and
    Managing Director: Mr. R. Indlekofer
Administration: Ms. M. Stebler
Titles published, 1972: 3

Telephone: (061) 35 85 00
Cable: Basiliuspresse
Founded: 1959

Titles in stock: 33
Subjects of books published: art, natural science

BASILIUS-PRESSE AG (cont'd)

Language of publications: German
Books distributed by: Heinz Moos Verlag, Hartnagelstrasse 11,
      8 Gräfeling vor München, Federal Republic of Germany;
      Anton Schroll & Co., Spengergasse 37, 1051 Vienna, Austria.

BENTELI VERLAG

Bümplizstrasse 101	Telephone: (031) 55 44 33
3018 Bern	Founded: 1899

Chairman of the Board: Mr. Ted Scapa
Titles published, 1972: 20   Titles in stock: 150
Subjects of books published: art, belles-lettres, humor
Language of publications: German

BENZIGER & CO. AG

Bellerivestrasse 3	Telephone: (01) 34 70 50
8008 Zurich	Telex: 54 545

Chairman of the Board: Dr. Karl Eberle   Cable: Benzigerco
Managing Director: Dr. Oscar Bettschart   Founded: 1792
Controller: Mr. Simon Kissling
Editor in Chief: Dr. Oscar Bettschart
Sales Director: Mr. Ferdinand Koller
Advertising Director: Mr. Hans Rühl
Titles published, 1972: 30   Titles in stock: 208
Subject of books published: theology
Language of publications: German
Distributor for: Johannes Verlag, Schaffhauserrheinweg 93, 4000
      Basel, Switzerland.

BIRCHER-BENNER-VERLAG

8703 Erlenbach-Zurich	Telephone: (051) 90 16 99
Managing Directors: Dr. Ralph Bircher	Founded: 1952

      and Mr. Günter Höpping Schwabe
Controller: Mr. Gerardus Kerst
Editor in Chief: Dr. Ralph Bircher
Advertising Director: Mr. A. Moser

BIRCHER-BENNER-VERLAG (cont'd)

Titles published, 1971: 3   Titles in stock: 42
Subjects of books published: health, nutrition, dietetics, psychotherapy
Language of publications: German
Distributor for: Helfer Verlag, Bad Homburg vdH; Editions Victor
     Attinger SA, Neuchâtel; Le Courrier du Livre, Paris.
Periodical: *Der Wendepunkt*, monthly ($8.00).

BIRKHAUSER VERLAG

     Elisabethenstrasse 19   Telephone: (061) 23 18 10
     4010 Basel   Telex: 63 475
Chairman of the Board: Mr. Albert Birkhäuser
Managing Director: Mr. Carl Einsele   Founded: 1879
Sales Director: Mr. Hans Jo Pfeiffer
Art Director: Mr. Albert Gomm
Titles published, 1972: 40   Titles in stock: 760
Subjects of books published: mathematics, natural sciences, art
Languages of publications: German, French, English
Books distributed by: Birkhäuser Verlag GmbH, Olgastrasse 53, 7000
     Stuttgart, Fed. Rep. of Germany; and Birkhäuser Verlag, Basel.
Periodicals: Birkhäuser publishes 19 scientific and mathematical
     journals. Most of these publications have multilingual texts
     (German, English, and French).

BLAUKREUZ-VERLAG

     Lindenrain 5a   Telephone: (031) 23 58 66
     3000 Bern 10   Founded: 1883
Chairman of the Board: Dr. H. Schaffner
Managing Director: Mr. Eduard Müller
Titles published, 1972: 10   Titles in stock: 110
Subjects of books published: belles-lettres, juvenile literature, religion,
     temperance literature
Language of publications: German
Periodicals: *Das Blaue Kreuz*, semi-monthly (SFr. 12.50); *Familienblatt*,
     monthly (SFr. 5); *Achtung . . . los!*, monthly (SFr. 5.50);
     Pflungschar, monthly (SFr. 12).

DIRECTORY

BUECHLER & CO. LTD.

Seftigenstrasse 310 — Telephone: (031) 54 11 11
3084 Wabern — Telex: 32 697 Bueco ch
Chairman of the Board: Prof. Hans Merz — Cable: Bupub Berne
Managing Director: Mr. Marc Büchler — Founded: 1966
Assistant Director: Mr. Wolfgang Johner
Controller: Ms. Anni Kiefer
Editor in Chief: Mr. Urs Gresly
Sales Director: Mr. Urs Graf
Advertising Director: Mr. Urs Graf
Rights and Permissions: Ms. Annemarie Amacher
Production Manager: Mr. Peter Steiger
Art Director: Mr. Urs Gresly
Titles published, 1971: 17 — Titles in stock: 45
Subjects of books published: art, juvenile literature, political science, education, picture books
Language of publications: German
Books distributed by: Swiss Books Center, Olten, Switzerland; F. A. Brockhaus, Stuttgart, Fed. Rep. of Germany; A. Huemer, Salzburg, Austria.
Periodicals: *Auto*, monthly (SFr. 25.10); *Der Motorlastwagen*, bi-weekly (SFs. 26.30); *Schweizer Technische Zeitschrift*, weekly (SFr. 49.10); *Illustrierte Schweizer Schülerzeitung*, monthly (SFr. 8.60); *Yachting*, monthly (SFr. 24).

WERNER CLASSEN VERLAG

Splügenstrasse 10 — Telephone: (01) 36 56 06
8027 Zurich — Founded: 1945
Subjects of books published: belles-lettres, poetry, music, art, juvenile literature, psychology
Language of publications: German

CONZETT & HUBER. *See* MANESSE VERLAG

DAPHNIS-VERLAG

Rebweg 3 — Telephone: (01) 90 06 39
8703 Erlenbach-Zurich — Founded: 1959

DAPHNIS-VERLAG (cont'd)

Managing Director: Mr. J. Fischlin
Titles published, 1971: 1   Titles in stock: 8
Subjects of books published: graphic art, and limited editions of
    special works
Language of publications: German

DELACHAUX & NIESTLE S.A.
    4, rue de l'Hôpital   Telephone: (038) 5 46 76
    2001 Neuchâtel   Founded: 1864
Chairman of the Board: Mr. Adolphe Niestlé
Managing Directors: Mr. Adolphe Niestlé and Mr. E. Chave
Assistant Director: Mr. D. Bròdariù
Controller: Mr. A. Muller
Sales Director: Mr. A. Delachaux
Advertising Director: Mr. D. Bròdariù
Rights and Permissions: Ms. F. Wirz
Titles published, 1971: 50
Subjects of books published: philosophy, psychology, theology, juvenile
    literature, medicine, science, mathematics, law, sociology
Language of publications: French
Bookstores owned by firm: Delachaux & Niestlé, 4, rue de l'Hôpital,
    2001 Neuchâtel.
Periodicals: *Binop*, quarterly

DELPHIN VERLAG
    Limmatstrasse 111   Telephone: (01) 44 07 33
    8031 Zurich   Telex: 53 815
                                       Cable: Delphinverlag Zurich
Titles published, 1971: 16   Founded: 1962
Subject of books published: juvenile literature
Language of publications: German

DIANA VERLAG
    Hadlaubstrasse 131   Telephone: (01) 26 48 50
    8006 Zurich   Founded: 1946

DIRECTORY

DIANA VERLAG (cont'd)

Managing Director: Dr. Simon Menzel

Subjects of books published: biography, history, philosophy, medicine, psychology

Language of publications: German

DIOGENES VERLAG AG

Sprecherstrasse 8   Telephone: (01) 47 89 47

8032 Zurich   Telex: 52 810

Chairman of the Board and Cable: Diogenes-verlag

   Managing Director: Mr. Daniel Keel   Zurich

Assistant Director: Mr. Rudolf C. Bettschart

Controller: Mr. Rudolf C. Bettschart   Founded: 1953

Editor in Chief: Mr. Daniel Keel

Sales Director: Mr. Hartmut Radel

Advertising Director: Mr. Hartmut Radel

Rights and Permissions: Ms. Ruth Binde

Production Manager: Mr. Rudolf C. Bettschart

Art Director: Mr. Hans Dörries

Titles published, 1972: 70   Titles in stock: 300

Subjects of books published: fiction, graphic art, juvenile literature

Language of publications: German (some graphic art books in English)

Books distributed by: Vereinigte Verlagsauslieferung, 83 Gütersloh, Friedrichsdorferstrasse 75, Fed. Rep. of Germany; Schweizer Buchzentrum, 4600 Olten, Switzerland; Rudolf Lechner & Sohn, Seilerstätte 5, 1010 Vienna, Austria; Ursula Sobottka, Sächsische Strasse 6, 1000 Berlin W. 15; Meulenhoff-Bruna N.V., Beulingstraat 2, Amsterdam C., Netherlands; Tysk Bogimport A.S., Vester Voldgade 83, Copenhagen, Denmark (for the Scandinavian countries).

GOTTLIEB DUTTWEILER INSTITUTE

Park "Im Grüene"   Telephone: (01) 724 00 20

Langhaldenstrasse 17   Telex: 55 699

8803 Rüschlikon-Zurich   Cable: Green Meadow

                            Founded: 1946

GOTTLIEB DUTTWEILER INSTITUTE (cont'd)

Managing director: Mr. H. A. Pestalozzi
Editors: Mr. R. Brun, Mr. H. Birenstihl, Mr. J. Cartwright
Advertising Director: Mr. Braune-Krickau
Titles published, 1973: 5   Titles in stock: 48
Subjects of books published: sociology, political science, economics
Languages of publications: English, French, German
Periodicals: *GDI-Information*, bi-weekly (SFr. 410.); *GDI-Topics*,
    monthly (SFr. 72.); *TED-Journal*, quarterly (SFr. 100.).

EDITA S.A.
3, rue de la Vigie   Telephone: (021) 20 56 31
1003 Lausanne   Cable: Editasa Lausanne
Chairman of the Board: Mr. Maurice Baumgartner
Managing Director: Mr. Ami Guichard   Founded: 1952
Controller: Mr. Gilbert Basset
Editor in Chief: Mr. Joseph Jobe
Art Director: Mr. Max Thommen
English Language Editor: Mr. Tim Chilvers
German Language Editor: Ms. Ursula Claren
Titles Published, 1972: 11   Titles in stock: 25
Subjects of books published: illustrated books on art, history, aviation,
    technology, navigation, automobiles
Languages of publications: French, English, German, Italian
Books distributed by: Office du Livre S.A., 101 Route de Villars,
    1700 Fribourg (in Switzerland). In other countries the firm
    works with co-publishers.
Periodicals: *Automobile Year*, annual (SFr. 42).

EDITIONS CLAIREFONTAINE. *See* LA GUILDE DU LIVRE

EDITIONS D'ART ALBERT SKIRA
4, Place du Molard   Telephone: (022) 25 72 50
1211 Geneva 3   Cable: Edart Geneva
Chairman of the Board and   Founded: 1928
    Managing Director: Mr. Albert Skira

EDITIONS D'ART ALBERT SKIRA (cont'd)

Controller: Mr. Jean-Michel Skira
Editor in Chief: Ms. Rosabianca Skira
Sales Director: Mr. Jean-Michel Skira
Rights and Permissions: Mr. Lauro Venturi
Production Manager: Mr. Henri Kunz
Art Director: Mr. Lauro Venturi
Titles published, 1972: 10   Titles in stock: 130
Subjects of books published: art (mainly painting), architecture,
    contemporary creative writing
Languages of publications: French, German, Italian, Spanish, English,
    and some multilingual texts
Books distributed by: Weber & Cie., 13, rue de Monthoux, 1200
    Geneva, and 90, rue de Rennes, Paris 6e, France (for all
    countries except the United States); Crown Publishers, Inc.,
    419 Park Ave. South, N.Y. 10016, N.Y. (for the United
    States on a non-exclusive basis).
Miscellaneous information: The firm is active in the field of co-produc-
    tions and has plans for cooperation with the Viking Press in
    New York.

EDITIONS DE LA BACONNIERE

2017 Boudry-Neuchâtel   Telephone: (031) 6 40 04
Chairman of the Board: Cable: Baconnière Boudry
    Dr. Hermann Hauser   Founded: 1927
Subjects of books published: belles-lettres, poetry, biography, history,
    music, art, philosophy, reference, psychology, social science,
    university textbooks
Language of publications: French

EDITIONS DELTA S.A.

40, Route de Chailly   Telephone: (021) 54 05 27
1814 La Tour-de-Peilz   Founded: 1963
Chairman of the Board: Mr. A. Van Gool
Managing Director: Mr. R. Galimont
Assistant Director: Mr. C. Ramseyer
Controller: Mr. R. Voumard

EDITIONS DELTA S.A. (cont'd)

Editor in Chief: Mr. R. Galimont
Rights and Permissions: Mr. R. Galimont
Production Manager and Art Director: Mr. A. Haeseldoucks
Titles published, 1972: 43   Titles in stock: 250
Subjects of books published: education, technology, science
Languages of publications: French, German, Italian

EDITIONS DROZ S.A.

11, rue Massot   Telephone: (022) 46 66 66
1211 Geneva 12   Founded: 1924

Chairman of the Board: Mr. Léon Dufour
Managing Director: Mr. Alain Dufour
Controller: Ms. Guéguen
Advertising Director: Mr. Christophe Senft
Titles published, 1972: 75   Titles in stock: 1,200
Subjects of books published: history of French literature, history,
    economics, philology, sociology
Languages of publications: French, German, Italian, English
Books distributed by: Minard, 73 rue du Cardinal Lemoine, Paris.
Periodicals: *Bibliothèque l'humanisme et renaissance*, 3 issues per year;
    Economies et sociétés, monthly; *Economie appliquée*, quarterly;
    Revue l'histoire des mines, annual; *Revue l'histoire de la banque*,
    annual.

EDITIONS DU GRIFFON

Place de la Gare 5   Telephone: (038) 7 94 30
2520 La Neuveville   Founded: 1944

Managing Director: Dr. Marcel Joray
Titles published, 1972: 7
Subjects of books published: art, science
Languages of publications: French, German, English (all art books
    are in English)

EDITIONS DU MONT-BLANC S.A.

72, rue de Lausanne   Telephone: (022) 31 52 10
1200 Geneva   Founded: 1946

EDITIONS DU MONT-BLANC S.A. (cont'd)

Chairman of the Board and Managing
     Director: Mr. Bernard Steele
Controller: Mr. Raymond Mory
Production Manager: Mr. René Pasche
Titles published, 1971: 6   Titles in stock: 56
Subjects of books published: psychology, religion, metaphysics,
     philosophy
Language of publications: French
Books distributed by: Office du Livre S.A., Route de Villars 101,
     1700 Fribourg, Switzerland; Editions Payot-Paris, 106, Blvd.
     Saint-Germain, Paris 6e, France

EDITIONS DU PANORAMA

2, rue d'Argent   Telephone: (032) 3 62 84
2500 Bienne   Founded: 1951
Chairman of the Board and Managing Director: Mr. Paul Thierrin
Titles published, 1972: 8
Subjects of books published: belles-lettres, gastronomy
Languages of publications: French, German, Italian
Books distributed by: Office du Livre, Route de Villars 101,
     1700 Fribourg, Switzerland; Editions Dunod, 92, rue
     Bonaparte, Paris 6e, France.

EDITIONS KISTER S.A.

33 Quai Wilson   Telephone: (022) 31 50 00
1200 Geneva   Telex: 27 168
Chairman of the Board: Mr. Pierre Kister   Cable: Kisteredit
Assistant Director: Mr. Thomas Fenwick   Founded: 1948
Sales Director: Mr. André Meister
Titles published, 1972: 20   Titles in stock: 60
Subjects of books published: encyclopedias, general reference
Languages of publications: French, German
Distributor for: IGDA (Istituto Geografico de Agostini), Novara,
     Italy; Grange-Batelière S.A., Paris, France.
Periodicals: *Alpha Encyclopédie*, weekly (SFr. 130); *Le Million*,

EDITIONS KISTER S.A. (cont'd)

> weekly (SFr. 130); *Les Muses*, weekly (SFr. 130); *La Faune*, weekly (SFr. 130).

Miscellaneous information: Kister's main operation at the present time is to distribute in Switzerland encyclopedias that are created or adapted by their sister firm in Paris.

EDITIONS LABOR ET FIDES

1, rue Beauregard	Telephone: (022) 24 21 25
1204 Geneva	24 21 50

Chairman of the Board: Prof. Jacques   Founded: 1924
    de Senarclens
Managing Director: Mr. Horace Lombard
Editor in Chief: Mrs. Ruth Welch
Titles published, 1972: 13   Titles in stock: 324
Subject of books published: Protestant theology
Language of publications: French
Distributor for: Editions du Scarabée, Paris, France.
Bookstore owned by firm: Librairie Labor et Fides, 1, rue Beauregard, 1204 Geneva.

EDITIONS L'AGE D'HOMME

10 Métropole	Telephone: (021) 22 00 95
Lausanne	Founded: 1966

Chairman of the Board: Mr. W. Dimitrijevic
Titles published, 1972: 35   Titles in stock: 130
Subjects of books published: theater, cinema, translations of classic Slavic and German works
Language of publications: French
Books distributed by: Librairie Hachette, 79, Boulevard Saint-Germain, Paris 6e, France (for Canada and the United States).
Bookstore owned by firm: La Proue, Lausanne
Periodicals: *Travail Théâtral*, quarterly.

LES EDITIONS NAGEL S.A.

5, rue de l'Orangerie	Telephone: (022) 34 17 30
1211 Geneva	Cable: Nageledit

LES EDITIONS NAGEL S.A. (cont'd)

Chairman of the Board: Mr. Louis Nagel   Founded: 1952
Titles published, 1972: 20   Titles in stock: 440
Subjects of books published: art, archaeology, philosophy, political
    science, literature, travel guides
Languages of publications: French, German, Italian, English, Russian,
    Greek, Danish, Serbo-Croatian
Books distributed by: Barrie & Jenkins Ltd., 2 Clement's Inn, Strand,
    London, W.C.2, England. (Other distributors in Austria, Belgium,
    Cyprus, Spain, Greece, Martinique, Iran, Turkey, Yugoslavia.)
Foreign Office: Les Editions Nagel S.A., 7, rue de Savoie, Paris 6e,
    France.
Periodicals: *Revue diplomatique*, monthly (SFr. 70).

EDITIONS PRO SCHOLA

29, rue des Terreaux   Telephone: (021) 23 66 55
1000 Lausanne 9   Cable: Dirbenedict
Managing Director: Mr. Jean J. Bénédict   Founded: 1928
Titles published, 1972: 3   Titles in stock: 60
Subjects of books published: language textbooks, workbooks
Languages of publications: French, German, Italian, Spanish, English
Miscellaneous information: This firm is closely related to, but still
    independent from, the International Bénédict Schools of
    Languages, which have branches in many countries in Western
    Europe.

EDITIONS RENCONTRE S.A.

29, chemin d'Entre-Bois   Telephone: (021) 32 38 41
1018 Lausanne   Telex: 24 876
Chairman of the Board: Mr. Pierre de   Cable: Rencontre Lausanne
    Muralt   Founded: 1928
Managing Director: Mr. François de Lorenzo
Editor in Chief: Mr. André de Muralt
Advertising Director: Mr. Albert Lorenzetti
Titles published, 1972: 256   Titles in stock: 1,500-2,000
Subjects of books published: belles-lettres, art, science
Languages of publications: French, German

PART B: PUBLISHING FIRMS

EDITIONS RENE KRAMER S.A.

48, Strada di Gandria	Telephone: (091) 51 89 41
6976 Castagnola	Founded: 1962

Chairman of the Board and Managing
    Director: Mr. René Kramer
Controller: Mr. Rudolf Wiederkehr
Production Manager: Mr. René Kramer
Titles published, 1972: 5   Titles in stock: 30
Subject of books published: gastronomy
Languages of publications: French, German, Italian, English

EDITIONS SPES S.A.

2 St. Pierre	Telephone: (021) 20 36 51
1000 Lausanne	Founded: 1917

Business Manager: Mr. Armand Bron
Editor in Chief: Mr. David Perret
Controller: Mr. Robert Bioley
Titles published, 1972: 25   Titles in stock: 110
Subjects of books published: education, science, technology
Language of publications: French
Books distributed by: Editions Bordas, 37, rue Boulard, 75 Paris 14e,
    France; Asedi, S.p.r.l., 102 chaussée de Charleroi, Bruxelles 6,
    Belgium.

EDITIONS UNIVERSITAIRES

39 Pérolles	Telephone: (037) 22 68 02
1700 Fribourg	Founded: 1953

Chairman of the Board: Dr. Hugo Baeriswyl
Sales Director: Dr. F. Rütsche
Titles published, 1972: 20   Titles in stock: 300
Subjects of books published: theology, law, philosophy, economics,
    history, science
Languages of publications: German, French, English, Italian

EDITO-SERVICE S.A.

37, rue Agasse	Telephone: (022) 35 72 33

EDITO-SERVICE S.A. (cont'd)

Case Postale 174
1211 Geneva 6

Telex: 22 971
Cable: Editoservice
Founded: 1963

Chairman of the Board: Mr. Georges F.
Perréard
Managing Director: Mr. Gaston Burnand
Controller: Mr. Hans Hauri
Editor in Chief: Mr. Gilbert Sigaux
Rights and Permissions: Ms. Yvonne Rosso
Production Manager: Mr. René Gioria
Art Director: Mr. Daniel Briffaud
Titles published, 1972: 480   Titles in stock: 2,000
Subjects of books published: classics, picture books, encyclopedias, travel, religion, biography, psychology, science, and special collections in luxury editions
Languages of publications: French, German, Italian, English, Norwegian, Danish, Dutch, Swedish, Finnish, Hebrew, Japanese
Books distributed by: Various book clubs all over the world.

ERKER-VERLAG

Gallusstrasse 32
9000 St. Gallen

Telephone: (071) 22 79 79
Founded: 1946

Chairman of the Board and Managing
Director: Mr. Franz Larese and Mr. Jürg Janett
Titles published, 1972: 8   Titles in stock: 38
Subject of books published: contemporary art
Languages of publications: German, French, English, Italian
Books distributed by: Weber & Cie, 13, rue Monthoux, 1201 Geneva.

EUROPA VERLAG AG

Rämistrasse 5
8001 Zurich

Telephone: (01) 47 16 29
Cable: Europaverlag
Founded: 1933

Titles published, 1971: 6   Titles in stock: 300
Subjects of books published: political science, history
Language of publications: German

EUROPA VERLAG AG (cont'd)

Distributor for: Europa Verlag, Vienna, Austria; UNESCO, Paris, France.

EX-LIBRIS VERLAG UND GRAMMOCLUB AG

Hermetschloostrasse 77	Telephone: (01) 62 51 00
8023 Zurich	Telex: 52 501
Chairman of the Board: Mr. Rudolf Suter	Founded: 1949

Managing Director: Dr. F. Lamprecht
Controller: Mr. Ernst Hochstrasser
Editor in Chief: Dr. Franz Lamprecht
Sales Director: Mr. Willy Bachmann
Advertising Director: Mr. Willy Toggwyler
Rights and Permissions: Dr. Georges Bollag
Production Manager: Mr. Oswald Dubacher
Art Director: Mr. Oswald Dubacher
Titles published, 1972: 250   Titles in stock: 1,067
Subjects of books published: juvenile literature, art, science, technology, belles-lettres
Languages of publications: French, German
Bookstores owned by firm: Firm owns 24 bookstores in the German and French speaking parts of Switzerland.
Book clubs owned by firm: Ex Libris
Periodicals: *Ex Libris*, monthly; *s'Zäni* (periodical for young people), 10 issues per year.

FABAG & DRUCKEREI WINTERTHUR AG

Industriestrasse 8	Telephone: (052) 29 44 21
8400 Winterthur	Founded: 1897

Chairman of the Board: Mr. N. Henggeler
Managing Director: Dr. R. Weber
Controller: Mr. J. Flury
Editor in Chief: Dr. H. R. Schneebeli
Sales Director: Mr. E. Furrer
Advertising Director: Dr. H. R. Schneebeli
Titles published, 1972: 3   Titles in stock: 25

FABAG & DRUCKEREI WINTERTHUR AG (cont'd)
Subjects of books published: architecture, arts and crafts, cook books
Languages of publications: German, French, English

FLAMBERG-VERLAG
Brauerstrasse 60	Telephone: (01) 23 28 63
8021 Zurich	Founded: 1958

Chairman of the Board: Mr. Jakob Guggisberg
Managing Director: Mr. Eugen Marti

Titles published, 1972: 20   Titles in stock: 90
Subjects of books published: fiction, political science, juvenile
    literature
Language of publications: German

FRANCKE VERLAG
Hochfeldstrasse 113	Telephone: (031) 23 74 68
3000 Bern 26	Telex: 32 326
Chairman of the Board and	Cable: Franckeverlag
Managing Director: Dr. C. L. Lang	Founded: 1831

Titles published, 1972: 60   Titles in stock: 1,200
Subjects of books published: Germanic and English philology,
    history, archaeology, philosophy, psychology, sociology,
    classical and romantic literature, music, textbooks, juvenile
    literature
Languages of publications: German, French, Italian, English
Bookstore owned by firm: Buchhandlung Francke, Neuengasse 43/
    von-Werdt-Passage, 3001 Bern.

GEORG & CIE S.A., LIBRAIRIES-EDITEURS
5 Corraterie	Telephone: (022) 26 13 55
1211 Geneva 11	Telex: 23 985
Chairman of the Board and	Founded: 1857
Managing Director: Mr. Henri Longchamp	

Titles published, 1971: 9   Titles in stock: 185
Subjects of books published: law, science
Language of publications: French

PART B: PUBLISHING FIRMS

GEORG & CIE S.A., LIBRAIRIES-EDITEURS (cont'd)

Bookstores owned by firm: Librairie de l'Université Georg & Cie., Geneva.

Miscellaneous information: The majority of this firm's publications are paperbacks.

GLOBI VERLAG

Eichstrasse 27
8045 Zurich
Managing Director: Mr. Emil Bannwart

Telephone: (01) 35 41 35
Telex: 52 791
Cable: Globiverlag
Founded: 1945

Titles published, 1973: 10
Subject of books published: juvenile literature
Language of publications: German

GOTTHELF-VERLAG

Badenerstrasse 69
8026 Zurich

Telephone: (01) 39 81 55
Founded: 1936

Chairman of the Board: Mr. E. Witzig
Managing Director: Mr. E. Ryser
Production Manager: Mr. E. Thiele
Titles published, 1972: 6   Titles in stock: 150
Subject of books published: theology
Languages of publications: German, English
Miscellaneous information: The firm is linked with the Methodist Church.

THE GRAPHIS PRESS, WALTER HERDEG

Nüschelerstrasse 45
8001 Zurich

Telephone: (01) 27 12 15
Cable: Graphispress

Editor and Art Director: Mr. Walter Herdeg Founded: 1944
Assistant Editor: Mr. Stanley Mason
Assistant to the Publisher: Mr. Jack J. Kunz
Business Manager; Mr. Gerhard Ruoss
Promotion and Advertising Manager: Mr. Harry Anderegg

THE GRAPHIS PRESS, WALTER HERDEG (cont'd)

Titles published, 1972: 7

Subjects of books published: advertising and applied art, advertising photography, graphic art, visual communications, posters

Languages of publications: All publications are in English, German, and French (multilingual texts).

Books distributed by: Hastings House Publishers, Inc., 10 E. 40th St., New York.

Periodicals: *Graphis: International Journal of Graphic Art and Applied Art*, bi-monthly ($23.50).

LA GUILDE DU LIVRE (Editions Clairefontaine)

4, Avenue de la Gare	Telephone: (021) 23 79 73
1003 Lausanne	Cable: GuildLivre Lausanne
Chairman of the Board: Mr. Charles-Henri Barbier	Founded: 1936

Managing Director: Mr. Albert Mermoud

Titles published, 1972: 28

Subjects of books published: fiction, art, mystery, juvenile literature, belles-lettres, history

Language of publications: French

Bookstores owned by firm: La Guilde du Livre, 43, rue du Bac, Paris 7e, France; La Guilde du Livre, 75, rue du Midi, Bruxelles, Belgium; La Guilde du Livre, 4, Avenue de la Gare, 1003 Lausanne, Switzerland.

Book club owned by firm: La Guilde du Livre.

Miscellaneous information: La Guilde du Livre was the first French-language book club to be founded in Europe.

TH. GUT & CO. VERLAG

8712 Stäfa-Zurich	Telephone: (01) 73 81 01
Chairman of the Board and	Founded: 1943
Managing Director: Mr. Ulrich Gut	

Assistant Director: Mr. Rudolf Frey

Editor in Chief: Mr. Ulrich Gut

Titles published, 1972: 4	Titles in stock: 28

Subjects of books published: history, culture

Languages of publications: German, some Swiss German

PART B: PUBLISHING FIRMS

BERCHTOLD HALLER VERLAG
Nägeligasse 9   Telephone: (031) 22 25 83
3000 Bern 7   Founded: 1848
Chairman of the Board: Mr. Paul Schär
Managing Director: Mr. Peter Schranz
Titles published, 1973: 3   Titles in stock: 75
Subject of books published: religion
Language of publications: German
Bookstores owned by firm: Buchhandlung der Evangelischen Gesellschaft, Nägeligasse 9, 3000 Bern 7; Evangelische Buchhandlung, Schmiedengasse 26, 3400 Burgdorf; Evangelische Buchhandlung, Melchaustrasse 8, 4900 Langenthal.

HALLWAG AG
Nordring 4   Telephone: (031) 42 31 31
3001 Bern   Telex: 32 460
Chairman of the Board and   Cable: Hallwag Bern
    Managing Director: Mr. O. E. Wagner Founded: 1912
Editor in Chief: Dr. P. Meyer
Sales Director: Dr. U. P. Thoenen
Rights and Permissions: Dr. P. Meyer
Production Manager: Mr. G. Noltkämper
Titles published, 1972: 20   Titles in stock: 282
Subjects of books published: travel, popular science, juvenile literature, art, road maps, atlases
Language of publications: German
Periodicals: *Automobile Revue*, weekly (SFr. 31.80); *Fertigung*, bi-monthly (SFr. 36); *Praxis*, weekly (SFr. 48.60); *Technische Rundschau*, weekly (SFr. 36); *Das Tier*, monthly (SFr. 24); *Unesco-Kurier*, monthly (SFr. 16).

PAUL HAUPT AG
Falkenplatz 14   Telephone: (031) 23 24 25
3001 Bern   Founded: 1906
Chairman of the Board and
    Managing Director: Mr. Paul Haupt
Editor in Chief: Mr. Paul Haupt

DIRECTORY

PAUL HAUPT AG (cont'd)

Advertising Director: Mr. U. Dodel
Production Manager; Mr. K. Thönnes
Titles published, 1971: 80   Titles in stock: 2,500
Subjects of books published: economics, finance, sociology, textbooks,
    political science, education
Languages of publications: German, French, Italian, English
Bookstores owned by firm: Paul Haupt AG, Falkenplatz 14, 3001
    Bern, and Länggasse 8, Bern.
Periodicals: *Ehe*, quarterly (SFr. 29); *Die Unternehmung*, quarterly
    (SFr. 33); *Körpererziehung*, monthly (SFr. 19); *Sportmedizin*,
    quarterly (SFr. 14).

HELBING & LICHTENHAHN
        Freiestrasse 40   Telephone: (061) 25 52 00
        4001 Basel   Cable: Heliba
Chairman of the Board and   Founded: 1822
        Managing Director: Mr. Heinz Helbing
Titles published, 1972: 30   Titles in stock: 600
Subjects of books published: law, history, textbooks
Languages of publications: German, English, French
Books distributed by: F. A. Brockhaus, Leberberg 25, 6200 Wies-
    baden, Fed. Rep. of Germany.
Bookstores owned by firm: Helbing & Lichtenhahn, Freiestrasse 40,
    4001 Basel; Piccolibro, Pfluggasse/Weissegasse, 4001 Basel.
Periodicals: *Praxis des Bundesgerichts*, monthly (SFr. 52); *Regio
    Basiliensis*, 2 issues per year (SFr. 17); *Zeitschrift für
    Schweizerisches Recht*, 8-10 issues per year (SFr. 66).

HELVETICA CHIMICA ACTA (Swiss Chemical Society)
        Postfach   Telephone: (061) 25 58 31
        4002 Basel   Founded: 1918
Chairman of the Board: Prof. E. Cherbuliez
Controller: Dr. R. Neher
Editor in Chief: Prof. E. Cherbuliez
Titles published, 1972: 9
Subject of books published: chemistry

PART B: PUBLISHING FIRMS

HELVETICA CHIMICA ACTA (cont'd)

Languages of publications: French, German, Italian, English (multi-lingual texts)

Books distributed by: Verlag Birkhäuser AG, Elisabethenstrasse 19, 4000 Basel.

Periodicals: *Helvetica Chimica Acta*, 9 issues per year ($40.90).

HANS HUBER PUBLISHERS

Länggasstrasse 76

3000 Bern 9

Telephone: (031) 24 25 33

Telex: 32 516

Chairman of the Board: Mr. Huber-Witz

Cable: Huberverlag

Managing Director: Mr. Walter Jäger

Founded: 1927

Controller: Mr. Röthlisberger

Editor in Chief: Mr. Heinz Weder

Sales Director: Mr. Max Pauli

Advertising Director: Mr. Walter Schürch

Rights and Permissions: Mr. Walter Jäger

Production Manager: Mr. Heinz Weder

Titles published, 1973: 70

Subjects of books published: medicine, psychology

Languages of publications: French, German, English

Books distributed by: Williams & Wilkins, Baltimore, Maryland.

Bookstores owned by firm: Buchhandlung Hans Huber, Marktgasse 9, 3000 Bern; Buchhandlung Hans Huber, Zeltweg 6, 8032 Zurich.

Periodicals: Huber publishes six periodicals in the medical sciences.

HUTHIG & WEPF VERLAG

Eisengasse 5

4000 Basel

Founded: 1947

Managing Directors: Dr. Alfred Huthig,
    Mr. Heinrich Wepf

Titles published, 1972: 2

Subject of books published: chemistry

Languages of publications: German, French, English

Bookstore owned by firm: Wepf & Co., Eisengasse 5, 4000 Basel.

DIRECTORY

IDES ET CALANDES S.A.
    19, Evole   Telephone: (038) 25 38 61
    2001 Neuchâtel   Cable: Idecal
Chairman of the Board and   Founded: 1941
    Managing Director: Mr. Fred Uhler
Controller: Ms. Bluette Sciboz
Editor in Chief: Mrs. Joan Rosselet
Production Manager: Mr. André Rosselet
Titles published, 1973: 6   Titles in stock: 80
Subjects of books published: art, law
Language of publications: French
Books distributed by: Office du Livre S.A., 101 Route de Villars,
    1700 Fribourg.

JURIS DRUCK & VERLAG AG
    Basteiplatz 5 / Talstrasse   Telephone: (01) 27 77 27
    8001 Zurich   Founded: 1945
Chairman of the Board: Dr. Hardy O. Christen
Managing Director: Mr. Josef Gasser
Assistant Director: Mr. Robert Konrad
Production Manager: Mr. Willy Grau
Titles published, 1972: 300   Titles in stock: 3,100
Subjects of books published: philosophy, psychology, law, agriculture,
    (theses in various subjects).
Languages of publications: German; occasionally French, English,
    Italian
Book club owned by firm: Juris Book Club.

KANISIUS VERLAG (Imba Verlag)
    4, Avenue de Beauregard
    1701 Fribourg   Founded: 1898
Publishing Directors: Dr. Michael Traber, Dr. Rolf Weibel
Titles published, 1972: 30   Titles in stock: 50
Subjects of books published: sociology, religion
Language of publications: German

PART B: PUBLISHING FIRMS

S. KARGER AG

    Arnold-Bröcklin-Strasse 25   Telephone: (061) 39 08 80

    4011 Basel   Telex: 62 652

Chairman of the Board and   Founded: 1890

    Managing Director: Mr. Thomas Karger, Dr. med. h. c.

Assistant Director: Mr. Roberto Zoppi

Sales and Promotion Manager: Mr. Andreas Straub

Rights and Permissions: Mr. Andreas Straub

Production Manager: Mr. Roberto Zoppi

Financial Manager: Mr. Peter Salathin

Titles published, 1973: 150

Subject of books published: biomedical sciences

Languages of publications: German, English (most publications are
    in English)

Books distributed by: S. Karger GmbH, Postfach 2, D-8034 Germering/
    Munich, Fed. Rep. of Germany; S. Karger S.A., 42bis, Boulevard
    de la Tour-Maubourg, F-75 Paris 7e, France; John Wiley and
    Sons Ltd., Baffins Lane, Chichester, Sussex, Great Britain;
    Albert J. Phiebig, Inc., P.O. Box 352, White Plains, N.Y. 10602,
    U.S.A.; Australasian Drug Information Services Pty. Ltd.,
    P.O. Box 194, Balgowlah, Sydney, N.S.W. 2093, Australia.

Bookstores owned by firm: Karger Libri AG, Petersgraben 14, 4000
    Basel.

Periodicals: Karger publishes 55 medical journals which are primarily
    in English. Some of these publications have multilingual texts
    (English, German, and French).

KORNFELD UND KLIPSTEIN

    Laupenstrasse 49   Telephone: (031) 25 46 73

    3000 Bern   Cable: Artus

Managing Director: Mr. Eberhard W.   Founded: 1864

    Kornfeld

Titles published, 1971: 5   Titles in stock: 10

Subject of books published: graphic art

Languages of publications: German, French

Books distributed by: Office du Livre S.A., 101 Route de Villars,
    1700 Fribourg.

DIRECTORY

KUMMERLY & FREY AG (GEOGRAPHISCHER VERLAG)

Hallerstrasse 6-12   Telephone: (031) 23 51 11
3001 Bern   Telex: 32 860
Managing Director: Mr. P. Etzweiler   Cable: Kümmerlyfrey
     Founded: 1852

Subjects of books published: geography, maps, picture books
Language of publications: German

KUNSTKREIS AG

Alpenstrasse 5   Telephone: (041) 23 59 12
6000 Lucerne   Telex: 78 276
Chairman of the Board: Dr. F. Emenegger   Cable: Kunstkreis Luzern
Managing Director: Mr. Walter Schweizer   Founded: 1947
Assistant Director: Mr. Urs Düggelin
Controller: Mr. Urs Düggelin
Editor in Chief: Dr. Louis Hertig
Sales Director: Mr. Urs Düggelin
Advertising Director: Mr. Walter Schweizer, Mr. Urs Düggelin
Production Manager: Mr. Jakob Schmidt
Titles published, 1972: 80   Titles in stock: 10 book series,
     14 single titles

Subjects of books published: art (painting, sculpture, architecture),
     history, encyclopedias
Languages of publications: French, German, English
Distributor for: Editions Rencontre, 29, Chemin d'Entre-Bois, 1018
     Lausanne; Ex Libris Verlag AG, Löwenstrasse 25, 8001 Zurich.
Periodicals: *Kunstnachrichten*, 10 issues per year (SFr. 12., or $8.50,
     air mail).
Miscellaneous information: This firm also publishes art prints, port-
     folios (containing six prints), posters, and original graphic art.

HERBERT LANG & CO. LTD.

Münzgraben 2   Telephone: (031) 22 17 08
3000 Bern 7   Telex: 33 173 lbook ch
Chairman of the Board: Mr. Herbert Lang   Cable: Herbertbook
Managing Directors: Dr. Ch. Lang, Mr.   Founded: 1921
     Peter Lang, Ms. L. Lang

HERBERT LANG & CO. LTD. (cont'd)

Assistant Directors: Mr. Hans Beutler, Mr. Otto Bareiss
Controller: Mr. Hanni Baumann
Editor in Chief: Mr. Diethard H. Klein
Sales Director: Mr. Robert Zimmerman
Advertising Director: Mr. Robert Zimmerman
Rights and Permissions: Mr. Peter Lang
Production Manager: Mr. Klaus Wolfgramm
Art Director: Mr. Klaus Wolfgramm
Titles published, 1972: 200   Titles in stock: 1,350
Subject of books published: science
Languages of publications: In most languages except the Scandinavian
    languages. Many are published in English.
Bookstore owned by firm: Herbert Lang & Cio., Münzgraben 2,
    3000 Bern 7.
Periodicals: *Schweizerische Versicherungszeitschrift*, monthly (SFr. 40);
    Orbis Scientiarum, quarterly (SFr. 18); *International Bibliog-*
    raphy on Insurance, quarterly (SFr. 50); *Ethnologische Zeit-*
    schrift, bi-annual (SFr. 28).

LIBRAIRIE PAYOT
    10, rue Centrale   Telephone: (021) 22 84 22
    1003 Lausanne   Telex: 24 953
Director: Mr. Jean-Pierre Payot   Founded: 1835
Subjects of books published: belles-lettres, poetry, history, music,
    art, general science, textbooks
Language of publications: French
Bookstores owned by firm: Payot has many bookstores in various
    cities all over Switzerland.
Foreign Office: Editions Payot, 106, Boulevard Saint-Germain,
    Paris 6e, France.

LA MAISON DE LA BIBLE
    Société Biblique de Genève
    11, rue de Rive
    1211 Geneva 3   Founded: 1917

LA MAISON DE LA BIBLE (cont'd)

Managing Director: Mr. Georges Berthoud
Assistant Director: Mr. Gottfried Wüthrich
Titles published, 1972: 3   Titles in stock: 50 (plus
                                            various editions of the
                                            Bible in 50 languages).
Subjects of books published: religion, philosophy, evangelistic
    literature
Languages of publications: French, German, Italian

MANESSE VERLAG (Conzett & Huber)
    Morgartenstrasse 29   Telephone: (01) 39 44 55
    8021 Zurich   Founded: 1944
Editor in Chief: Dr. Federico Hindermann
Titles published, 1973: 9   Titles in stock: 250
Subject of books published: belles-lettres
Language of publications: German

ALBERT MULLER VERLAG AG
    Bahnhofstrasse 69   Telephone: (01) 724 17 60
    8803 Rüschlikon-Zurich   Telex: 563 20 Amv ch
Chairman of the Board and Managing   Cable: Muellerverlag
    Director: Mr. Adolf Recher-Vogel Founded: 1936
Assistant Director: Mr. Anton Hegglin
Editor in Chief: Dr. Marta Jacober
Advertising Director: Mr. Bernard Recher-Berthold
Rights and Permissions: Mr. Anton Hegglin
Production Manager: Ms. Ursula Merkle
Titles published, 1973: 35   Titles in stock: 350
Subjects of books published: juvenile literature, general non-fiction
    (gardening, sports, cooking, health), popular science
Languages of publications: German, French

MULTILING VERLAG AG
    Hufgasse 17   Telephone: (01) 47 33 29
    8008 Zurich   Founded: 1972

MULTILING VERLAG AG (cont'd)

Managing Director: Dr. Ulrich Bär
Titles published, 1972: 1   Titles in stock: 1
Subjects of books published: multilingual texts, reference
Languages of publications: French, German, English, Spanish

MUNZEN UND MEDAILLEN AG

Malzgasse 25   Telephone: (061) 23 75 44
4002 Basel   Cable: Monnaies Bâle
Directors: Mr. Herbert A. Cahn,   Founded: 1942
    Mr. Erich B. Cahn, Mr. Pierre Strauss
Titles published, 1971: 4   Titles in stock: 15
Subject of books published: numismatics
Language of publications: German

NEUE ZEITSCHRIFT FUR MISSIONSWISSENSCHAFT

6375 Schöneck / Beckenried   Telephone: (041) 84 52 07
Chairman of the Board: Dr. J. Mesot   Founded: 1945
Managing Director: Dr. J. Specker
Assistant Director: Dr. J. Zürcher
Controller: Dr. J. Specker
Editor in Chief: Dr. J. Beckmann
Sales Director: Dr. J. Specker
Production Manager: Dr. J. Specker
Titles published, 1972: 2   Titles in stock: 36
Subject of books published: missiology
Languages of publications: French, German, Italian
Periodicals: *Neue Zeitschrift für Missionswissenschaft (Nouvelle Revue de Science Missionaire)*, quarterly ($5.00).

ARTHUR NIGGLI LTD.

9052 Niederteufen   Telephone: (071) 33 17 72
Chairman of the Board: Ms. Ida Niggli Cable: Niggliverlag
Managing Director: Mr. Arthur Niggli Founded: 1950
Controller: Mr. Robert Riklin
Titles published, 1972: 28   Titles in stock: 90

ARTHUR NIGGLI LTD., (cont'd)

Subjects of books published: modern art (mainly graphic prints), architecture, visual communication, typography, printing techniques
Languages of publications: German, English, French (usually multilingual texts)
Distributor for: Verlag Gerd Hatje, Stuttgart; Phaidon-Verlag, Cologne, Fed. Rep. of Germany.

NORD-SUD VERLAG

Usterstrasse 737	Telephone: (01) 86 91 94
8617 Mönchaltdorf	Cable: Nordsüd
Managing Directors: Mr. Dimitrije	Founded: 1960
Sidjanski, Ms. Brigitte Sidjanski	
Titles published, 1972: 15	Titles in stock: 43

Subjects of books published: high quality children's picture books
Languages of publications: French, German, Italian, Dutch, Africaans, Danish, Finnish, Spanish, Japanese, Swedish
Books distributed by: Verlag Die Waage, Langwattstrasse 22, 8125 Zurich-Zollikerberg, Switzerland.
Miscellaneous information: This small family firm has won several prizes in Europe for children's books.

EMIL OESCH VERLAG AG

Seestrasse 3	Telephone: (01) 720 13 33
8800 Thalwil	Founded: 1932
Chairman of the Board: Mr. Emil Oesch	
Managing Director: Ms. Marianna K. Möbis	
Editor in Chief: Mr. Emil Oesch	
Advertising Director: Ms. Marianna K. Möbis	
Titles published, 1972: 4	Titles in stock: 60

Subject of books published: economics
Language of publications: German

OFFICE DU LIVRE S.A.

101 Route de Villars	Telephone: (037) 24 07 44
1700 Fribourg	Telex 36 227

OFFICE DU LIVRE S.A. (cont'd)

Chairman of the Board: Mr. Louis de Chollet

Managing Director: Mr. Jean Hirschen

Assistant Director: Mr. Pierre Engel

Controller: Mr. Paul Spillmann

Editors in Chief: Mr. Henri Hillebrand and Mr. Didier Coigny

Sales Director: Mr. Jean Hirschen

Advertising Director: Mr. Pierre Engel

Rights and Permissions: Mr. Jean Hirschen

Production Manager: Mr. Franz Stadelmann

Titles published, 1972: 19

Subjects of books published: art, hobbies

Languages of publications: French, German, Italian, Spanish, English, Japanese

Miscellaneous information: This firm acts as a distributor for numerous publishers in Switzerland, France, and Germany.

Cable: Livroffice

Founded: 1946

Titles in stock: 100

ORELL FUSSLI VERLAG

Nüschelerstrasse 22

8022 Zurich

Managing Director: Mr. Max Hofmann

Sales Director: Mr. Walter Köpfli

Subjects of books published: general fiction, belles-lettres, history, music, art, juveniles, aeronautics, automobile

Language of publications: German

Telephone: (051) 25 36 36

Cable: Füssliverlag

Founded: 1519

OTT VERLAG THUN

Länggasse 57

3601 Thun

Editor in Chief: Mr. Walter Knecht

Sales Manager: Mr. Nino D'Andrea

Advertising Director: Mr. Marco de Roche

Rights and Permissions: Mr. Marc de Roche

Technical Director: Mr. Sepp Lanz

Titles published, 1973: 18

Telephone: (033) 2 11 12

Cable: Ott

Founded: 1923

Titles in stock: 72

OTT VERLAG THUN (cont'd)

Subjects of books published: general non-fiction, science
Language of publications: German
Bookstore owned by firm: Verlags und Versandbuchhandlung Thun AG,
    Länggasse 57, 3601 Thun.
Periodicals: *IZA—Illustrierte Zeitschrift für Arbeitsschutz*, bi-monthly
    (SFr. 11).

PANTON-VERLAG

Restelbergstrasse 71   Telephone: (01) 26 22 44
8044 Zurich   Founded: 1961

Subjects of books published: belles-lettres, poetry, music, psychology,
    juvenile literature

PHAROS VERLAG HANSRUDOLF SCHWABE AG

St. Alban-Vorstadt 49   Telephone: (061) 23 27 09
4002 Basel   Founded: 1958

Chairman of the Board and Managing
    Director: Dr. Hansrudolf Schwabe
Titles published, 1973: 14   Titles in stock: 60
Subjects of books published: ethnology, juvenile literature, books on
    Switzerland and Basel
Language of publications: German
Bookstore owned by firm: Buchhandlung Münsterberg Hansrudolf
    Schwabe AG, Münsterberg 13, 4002 Basel.

RABER VERLAG AG

Frankenstrasse 9   Telephone: (041) 22 74 22
6002 Lucern   Founded: 1832

Chairman of the Board: Mr. B. L. Raeber
Managing Director: Mr. R. Räber-Huber
Titles published, 1973: 2   Titles in stock: 80
Subjects of books published: mathematics, religion
Language of publications: German

PART B: PUBLISHING FIRMS

FRIEDRICH REINHARDT VERLAG

Missionstrasse 36   Telephone: (061) 25 33 90
4000 Basel 12   Cable: Freinhardt Basel
Chairman of the Board: Dr. Marcus Löw   Founded: 1900
Managing Director: Dr. Ernst Reinhardt
Assistant Director: Mr. Herbert Denecke
Controller: Mr. Max W. Heyer
Editor in Chief: Dr. Ernst Reinhardt
Sales Director: Mr. Paul Minder
Advertising Director: Mr. Herbert Denecke
Rights and Permissions: Dr. Ernst Reinhardt
Production Manager: Mr. Herbert Denecke
Art Director: Mr. Karl-Heiner Preiswerk
Titles published, 1972: 20   Titles in stock: 300
Subjects of books published: fiction, biography, theology, juvenile
     literature, biology
Languages of publications: German; a few are published in English
Distributor for: Ernst Kaufmann KG, Alleestrasse 2, 7630 Lahr,
     Fed. Rep. of Germany
Periodicals: *Theologische Zeitschrift*, semi-monthly (SFr. 43);
     Kirchenblatt für die reformierte Schweiz, semi-monthly (SFr.
     35.50); *Basler Predigten*, monthly (SFr. 10).

EUGEN RENTSCH VERLAG

Wiesenstrasse 48   Telephone: (01) 90 01 33
8703 Erlenbach-Zurich   Founded: 1911
Chairman of the Board and Managing
     Director: Dr. Eugen Rentsch
Advertising Director: Dr. L. Rentsch
Rights and Permissions: Dr. E. Rentsch
Titles published, 1971: 6   Titles in stock: 450
Subjects of books published: history, social science, school books,
     psychology, philosophy
Language of publications: German

REX-VERLAG

St. Karliquai 12   Telephone: (041) 22 69 12
Postfach 161   Founded: 1931
6000 Lucerne 5

REX-VERLAG (cont'd)

Managing Director: Dr. Zeno Inderbitzin
Subjects of books published: education, juvenile literature, religion,
belles-lettres
Language of publications: German
Books distributed by: Faehrmann-Verlag, Vienna, Austria; F. A.
Brockhaus, 7 Stuttgart, Fed. Rep. of Germany.
Distributor for: Faehrmann-Verlag, Vienna, Austria; Haus Altenberg,
Duesseldorf; Don Bosco-Verlag, Munich (both in Fed. Rep. of
Germany).
Bookstore owned by firm: Rex-Buchhandlung, St. Karliquai 12,
6000 Lucern 5.

RODANA VERLAG. *See* SCHWEIZER SPIEGEL VERLAG

ROTH & SAUTER S.A.
25 rue du Simplon   Telephone: (021) 26 31 33
1006 Lausanne   Founded: 1906
Chairman of the Board: Mr. Max-François Roth
Managing Director: Mr. Michel Logoz
Assistant Director: Mr. Félix Monnier
Controller: Mr. Bernard Longchamp
Editor in Chief: Mr. Pierre Sauter
Titles published, 1972: 1   Titles in stock: 10
Subject of books published: illustrated books on fine art
Language of publications: French

SANSSOUCI VERLAG
Rosenbühlstrasse 37   Telephone: (01) 34 21 54
8044 Zurich   Founded: 1943
Managing Director: Mr. Peter Schifferli   Titles in stock: 270
Subjects of books published: how-to, general non-fiction
Language of publications: German
Books distributed by: Sanssouci Verlag, Erikastrasse 11, 8003
Zurich.

SAUERLANDER AG

Laurenzenvorstadt 89   Telephone: (064) 22 12 64
5001 Aarau   Cable: Sauerländer Verlag
Chairman of the Board: Mr. H. R. Sauer-   Founded: 1807
länder
Titles published, 1972: 25
Subjects of books published: juvenile literature, picture books,
chemistry, medicine, textbooks
Language of publications: German
Books distributed by: Sauerländer & Co., Finkenhofstrasse 21, 6000
Frankfurt, Fed. Rep. of Germany; Danubia-Verlag Universitäts-
buchhandlung, Wilhelm Braumüller & Sohn, GmbH., Rechte
Wienzeile 97, Vienna, Austria
Periodicals: *Gesnerus*, quarterly; *Cockpit*, monthly; *Chimia* (in
German, French, and English), monthly.

SCHERZ VERLAG AG

Marktgasse 25   Telephone: (031) 22 68 33
3000 Berne   Telex: 32 552
Chairman of the Board and Managing   Cable: Scherzedit
Director: Mr. Rudolf Streit-Scherz   Founded: 1939
Editor: Ms. Ursula Ibler
Sales Director: Mr. Elmar Send
Advertising Director: Mr. Günter Scholz
Rights and Permissions: Ms. Ursula Griessel
Production Manager: Mr. Hans Bettschart
Art Director: Mr. Günter Scholz
Titles published, 1971: 129
Subjects of books published: political science, documentaries, fiction,
history, biography, mystery, general non-fiction
Language of publications: German
Books distributed by: Schweizer Buchzentrum, Olten; Rudolf Lecher
& Sohn, Seilerstaette 5, Vienna 1, Austria.

SCHRITT VERLAG

6515 Cugnasco   Telephone: (092) 6 90 42
                              Cable: Dürr Cugnasco

SCHRITT VERLAG (cont'd)

Managing Director: Dr. Charles Dürr   Founded: 1945
Titles published, 1972: 4   Titles in stock: 15
Subjects of books published: Swiss law, Swiss art, economics
Languages of publications: French, German

SCHULTHESS POLYGRAPHISCHER VERLAG AG

    Zwingliplatz 2   Telephone: (01) 34 93 36
    8001 Zurich   Founded: 1791
Chairman of the Board: Dr. Albers
Managing Director: Mr. B. Waldburger
Editor in Chief: Mr. E. Rüegger
Titles published, 1972: 20
Subjects of books published: law, textbooks
Languages of publications: German; occasionally English
Distributor for: Rudolf Müller Verlagsgesellschaft, Stolbergerstrasse 84,
    5000 Köln-Braunsfeld, Fed. Rep. of Germany.

SCHWABE & CO.

    Steinentorstrasse 13   Telephone: (061) 23 55 23
    4000 Basel 10   Cable: Schwabeco
Chairman of the Board and Managing   Founded: 1494
    Director: Dr. Christian Overstolz
Manager: Mr. Hans Reimann
Controller: Mr. M. Götz
Editor in Chief: Dr. H. G. Oeri
Sales Manager: Mr. M. Götz
Advertising Manager: Mr. R. Kruker
Rights and Permissions: Dr. R. C. Cackett
Production Manager: Mr. J. Niederberger
Titles published, 1971: 30   Titles in stock: 570
Subjects of books published: medicine, philosophy
Languages of publications: German, French, English
Periodicals: *Acta Paedopsychiatrica*, monthly (SFr. 75, plus postage);
    Bulletin der Schweizerischen Akademie der Medizinischen
    Wissenschaften, six issues (SFr. 48, plus postage); *Helvetica*

PART B: PUBLISHING FIRMS

SCHWABE & CO. (cont'd)

Chirurgica Acta, six issues (SFr. 90, plus postage); *Helvetica Medica Acta*, six issues (SFr. 66, plus postage); *Helvetica Paediatrica Acta*, six issues (SFr. 90, plus postage); *Museum Helveticum*, four issues (SFr. 28, plus postage); *Schweizerische Medizinische Wochentschrift*, weekly (SFr. 54, plus postage); *Schweizerische Zeitschrift für Gynäkologie und Geburtschilfe*, six issues (SFr. 80, plus postage); *Schweizerische Zeitschrift für Militärmedizin*, four issues (SFr. 10, plus postage).

SCHWEIZER JUGEND—VERLAG

Weissensteinstrasse 2	Telephone: (065) 2 75 21
4500 Solothurn	Founded: 1886

Chairman of the Board: Mr. Josef P. Specker
Managing Director: Mr. Paul E. Schwarz

Titles published, 1973: 12	Titles in stock: 120

Subject of books published: education, juvenile literature
Language of publications: German
Periodicals: *Schweizer Jugend*, weekly (SFr. 47.40).

SCHWEIZER SPIEGEL VERLAG AG (Rodana Verlag)

Hirschengraben 20	Telephone: (01) 47 21 95
Postfach 144	(01) 32 34 32
8024 Zurich	Founded: 1925

Chairman of the Board: Dr. P. V. Huggler
Assistant Directors: Mr. M.-L. Davi and C. Davi
Editor in Chief: Dr. N. Flüeler
Sales Director: Mr. W. Knecht
Advertising Director: Mr. W. Knecht
Rights and Permissions: Dr. D. Roth

Titles in stock: 75

Subjects of books published: Swiss history, Swiss cooking, child psychology, juvenile literature
Languages of publications: English, German, Italian
Books distributed by: Ott Verlag AG, Länggasse 57, 3601 Thun, Switzerland.

DIRECTORY

SCHWEIZER VERLAGSHAUS AG

Klausstrasse 33
8008 Zurich
Chairman of the Board: Mr. Carl Meyer
Managing Director: Dr. Armin Meyer

Telephone: (01) 34 04 53
(01) 34 04 89
Telex: 53 514 svh ch
Cable: Druckverlaghaus
Founded: 1907

Titles published, 1971: 10   Titles in stock: 168
Subjects of books published: fiction, juvenile literature, animal books
Language of publications: German
Book club owned by firm: Neue Schweizer Bibliothek, Klausstrasse 33, 8008 Zurich.

SCRIPTAR S.A.

23, avenue de la Gare
1000 Lausanne
Chairman of the Board: Mr. G. F. Waefler

Telephone: (021) 20 23 51
Telex: 24 543
Cable: Orlog
Founded: 1934

Titles published, 1971: 12
Subjects of books published: horology, jewelry, incision engineering, technology
Languages of publications: French, German, English, Spanish
Periodicals: *Journal Suisse d'Horlogerie et de Bijouterie*, monthly; *Schweizerische Uhrmacher-Zeitung*, monthly; *Schweizer Goldschmied*, monthly; *Microtecnic*, 8 issues per year.

SINWEL-VERLAG

Gerberngasse 16
Postfach 9
3000 Bern 8   Founded: 1964
Titles published, 1971: 2   Titles in stock: 40
Subjects of books published: fiction, political science
Language of publications: German
Distributor for: Erich Röth Verlag, Mariental 36, Eisenach, German Democratic Republic.

PART B: PUBLISHING FIRMS

SPEER-VERLAG
Hofstrasse 134
8044 Zurich
Chairman of the Board: Dr. R. Römer

Telephone: (01) 32 12 03
Cable: Speerverlag
Founded: 1944
Titles in stock: 53

Subjects of books published: poetry, fiction, juvenile literature
Language of publications: German

STAUFFACHER-VERLAG AG
Birmensdorferstrasse 318
8055 Zurich
Chairman of the Board and Managing
    Director: Dr. Eugen Th. Rimli
Editor in Chief: Mr. Karl Fischer
Production Manager: Mr. Jürgen Kleger
Titles published, 1972: 34

Telephone: (01) 35 51 60
Cable: Stauffacheredit
Founded: 1923

Titles in stock: 210

Subjects of books published: art, popular science, classics, tourist
    guides
Languages of publications: French, German, Dutch

SWEDENBORG VERLAG
Apollostrasse 2
Postfach 247
8032 Zurich
Chairman of the Board: Dr. Edwin Frehner
Managing Director: Dr. Friedemann Horn
Controller: Ms. H. Frehner
Editor in Chief: Dr. Friedemann Horn
Titles published, 1972: 5

Founded: 1952

Titles in stock: 50

Subject of books published: religion
Language of publications: German

THEOLOGISCHER VERLAG
Brauerstrasse 60
8021 Zurich
Chairman of the Board: Mr. Jakob Guggisberg

Telephone: (01) 23 39 38
Founded: 1971

DIRECTORY

THEOLOGISCHER VERLAG (cont'd)

Managing Director: Mr. Eugen Marti
Assistant Director: Mr. Marcel Pfändler
Titles published, 1972: 45   Titles in stock: 620
Subject of books published: theology
Language of publications: German
Bookstores owned by firm: Evangelische Buchhandlung, Zurich;
    Nova-Buchhandlung, Zurich; Nova-Buchhandlung, Uster;
    Nova-Buchhandlung, Wetzikon; Evangelische Buchhandlung,
    Chur (all in Switzerland).
Periodicals: *Musik und Gottesdienst*, bi-monthly (SFr. 20); *Judaica*,
    quarterly (SFr. 18).
Miscellaneous information: This firm was founded as a result of the
    merger of the Zurich-based firms, EVZ-Verlag and Editio
    Academica.

URS GRAF VERLAG GmbH

Hasenbergstrasse 7   Telephone: (01) 88 44 44
8953 Dietikon-Zurich   Founded: 1940
Subject of books published: art, scholarly works, high-priced
    facsimiles
Language of publications: German

VERBANDSDRUCKEREI AG. BERN

Maulbeerstrasse 10   Telephone: (031) 25 29 11
3001 Bern   Telex: 32 255
Chairman of the Board: Mr. Hans Tschanz   Cable: Verbandsdruck
Managing Director: Mr. Werner Ellen-   Founded: 1919
    berger
Assistant Director: Mr. Robert Hirsiger
Publishing Director: Mr. Otto B. Jost
Production Manager: Mr. Adolf Haenni
Titles published, 1972: 7   Titles in stock: 70
Subjects of books published: agriculture, geography, juvenile litera-
    ture, women, almanacs, picture books
Languages of publications: German, French, Italian, English

VERLAG C. J. BUCHER AG

Zürichstrasse 3-9
6003 Lucerne
Chairman of the Board: Ms. Alice Bucher
Managing Director: Mr. Jürgen
    Braunschweiger
Controller: Mr. Louis Bäurle
Editor in Chief: Dr. Xavier Schnieper
Sales Director: Mr. Heinz Jansen
Advertising Director: Mr. Heinz Jansen
Rights and Permissions: Ms. Heidrun Diltz
Production Manager: Mr. Hans-Peter Renner

Telephone: (041) 24 11 44
Telex: 78 123
Cable: Cibag
Founded: 1861

Titles published, 1972: 35   Titles in stock: 120
Subjects of books published: art, biography, history, picture books
Languages of publications: French, German, Italian, English
Bookstore owned by firm: Löwenbuchhandlung, Lucerne.
Periodicals: *Camera-Magazine*, monthly ($18.00).

VERLAG DER NEUE BUND

Postfach
8025 Zurich
Chairman of the Board: Mr. Jakob Manz
Managing Director: Mr. Jakob Ragaz

Telephone: (01) 32 76 44
Founded: 1940

Titles in stock: 10
Subjects of books published: ethics, politics, social issues
Language of publications: German
Miscellaneous information: This firm was founded by the Escherbund,
    an association for a free, democratic socialism and international
    solidarity.

VERLAG DIE PFORTE

Blauensteinerstrasse 5
4053 Basel
Chairman of the Board and Managing
    Director: Dr. C. Schachenmann

Telephone: (061) 35 13 12
Founded: 1951

Titles published, 1971: 5
Subjects of books published: philosophy, belles-lettres
Languages of publications: German

DIRECTORY

VERLAG DIE WAAGE

Langwattstrasse 22
8125 Zollikerberg-Zurich
Chairman of the Board: Mr. Felix M. Wiesner
Titles published, 1971: 7
Subjects of books published: philosophy, orientalism
Language of publications: German
Distributor for: Nord-Süd Verlag, Usterstrasse 737, 8617 Mönchalt-
dorf; Cecilie Dressler Verlag, 1000 Berlin 15, Meinekestrasse
13, Fed. Rep. of Germany; Herold Verlag Brück KG, Stutt-
gart; Schneekluth Verlag, Munich; L. Staackmann Verlag,
Munich, Fed. Rep. of Germany.

Telephone: (051) 63 72 23
Founded: 1951

Titles in stock: 40

VERLAG MAX BINKERT & CO.

Postfach 32
4335 Laufenburg
Chairman of the Board and Managing
Director: Mr. Max Binkert
Assistant Director: Mr. Hans Jegge
Editor in Chief: Mr. Max Binkert
Titles published, 1972: 2
Subjects of books published: packaging, materials, handling
Language of publications: German
Periodicals: *Betriebsführung—Büro und Informationstechnik*, monthly
(SFr. 32); *Bürotechnische Praxis*, bi-monthly; *Grafiscope*,
bi-monthly; *Polyscope Automatik & Elektronik*, monthly.

Telephone: (064) 64 17 77
Cable: Mabico
Founded: 1952

VERLAG HUBER & CO. AG

Promenadenstrasse 16
8500 Frauenfeld
Managing Director: Mr. Manfred Vischer
Assistant Director: Mr. Rudolf Pfister
Sales Director: Mr. Hansrudolf Frey
Production Manager: Mr. Rolf A. Stähli
Titles published, 1971: 25
Subjects of books published: history, military science, textbooks,
belles-lettres

Telephone: (054) 7 27 50
Founded: 1809

Titles in stock: 300

VERLAG HUBER & Co. AG (cont'd)

Language of publications: German
Bookstore owned by firm: Buchhandlung Huber & Co. AG, 8500 Frauenfeld
Distributor for: Siegler & Co., Verlag für Zeitarchive GmbH, Bonn, Fed.
    Rep. of Germany.
Periodicals: *Allgemeine Schweizerische Militärzeitschrift*, monthly
    (SFr. 25).

VERLAG HELMUT KOSSODO

15, rue de la Cité   Telephone: (022) 26 48 80
1204 Geneva   Founded: 1952
Chairman of the Board and Managing
    Director: Mr. Helmut Kossodo
Titles published, 1972: 6   Titles in stock: 45
Subject of books published: belles-lettres
Language of publications: German

VERLAG LEEMANN AG

Buchdruckerei und Verlag   Telephone: (01) 34 66 50
Arbenzstrasse 20   Founded: 1893
8008 Zurich
Subjects of books published: aerodynamics, geodetics, hydraulics,
    structural statistics, textile engineering, thermodynamics
Languages of publications: French, German, Italian, English
Books distributed by: Stechert-Hafner, Inc., New York.
Miscellaneous information: This firm publishes publications of the
    Swiss Federal Institute of Technology.

VERLAG SCHIFFAHRT UND WELTVERKEHR AG

Blumenrain 12   Telephone: (061) 25 75 00
Postfach   Cable: Worldtrafic
4001 Basel   Founded: 1946
Chairman of the Board: Mr. Theo Zingg
Managing Director: Mr. Albin Breitenmoser
Editor in Chief: Mr. Albin Breitenmoser
Titles published, 1971: 2   Titles in stock: 90

VERLAG SCHIFFAHRT UND WELTVERKEHR AG (cont'd)

Subjects of books published: shipping and tourism on the Rhine
and other rivers
Languages of publications: German, French, English
Periodicals: *Strom und See*, monthly (SFr. 30).

VERLAG STAMPFLI & CIE. AG

Hallerstrasse 7-9
3001 Bern
Chairman of the Board and Managing
Director: Dr. Jakob Stämpfli
Assistant Director: Mr. Klaus Zeller
Editor in Chief: Dr. Jakob Stämpfli
Sales Director: Ms. Ruth Dennler
Advertising Director: Mr. Klaus Zeller
Titles published, 1972: 30   Titles in stock: 550
Subjects of books published: law, history, archaeology, art
Languages of publications: German, French
Books distributed by: F. A. Brockhaus Co., Ltd., Leberberg 25,
6200 Wiesbaden, Fed. Rep. of Germany.
Periodicals: *Schweizerische Zeitschrift für Sozialversicherung*,
quarterly (SFr. 52); *Schweizerische Zeitschrift für Strafrecht
(Revue Pénale Suisse)*, quarterly (SFr. 48); *Zeitschrift des
Bernischen Juristenvereins*, monthly (SFr. 34).

Telephone: (031) 23 23 23
Telex: 32 950 ch
Cable: Buchstaempfli Bern
Founded: 1799

A & S VOGEL VERLAG

9053 Teufen   Founded 1922
Chairman of the Board: Dr. A. Vogel
Assistant Director: Mr. M. Wohlers
Titles published, 1972: 1
Subject of books published: health
Languages of publications: German, French, English, Swedish,
Finnish, Spanish, Dutch
Periodicals: *Gesundheitsnachrichten / Health News*, in German and
Finnish, monthly; in French and English, quarterly (SFr. 8.50,
SFr. 10, abroad).

WALTER-VERLAG AG

Amthausquai 21

4600 Olten

Managing Director: Dr. J. Rast

Production Manager: Mr. H. Theo Frey

Telephone: (062) 21 76 21

Telex: 68 226

Cable: Walterverlag Olten

Founded: 1921

Titles in stock: 400

Subjects of books published: psychology, philosophy, literature, theology, travel guides, picture books

Language of publications: German

Periodicals: *Die Woche*, weekly (SFr. 37); *Der Sonntag*, weekly (SFr. 37).

ADDRESSES OF ORGANIZATIONS

PRESS

Centre de Recherche et de Promotion de la Presse Suisse (PPS)
   21, avenue de la Gare
   1002 Lausanne

BOOK TRADE

Schweizerischer Buchhändler-und Verleger-Verein (SBVV)
   Bellerivestrasse 3
   8008 Zurich

Société des Librairies et Editeurs de la Suisse Romande
   2, avenue Agassiz
   1001 Lausanne

SELECTED BIBLIOGRAPHY

BOOKS

Hartmann, Frederick H. *The Swiss Press and Foreign Affairs in World War II.* Gainesville, Florida: University of Florida Press, 1960.

Huber, Hans. *How Switzerland Is Governed.* Zurich: Schweizer Spiegel Verlag, 1968.

Hürlimann, Martin, ed. *Der Schweizer Verlag.* Zurich: Schweizerischer Buchhändler-und Verleger-Verein, 1961.

McRae, Kenneth D. *Switzerland: Example of Cultural Coexistence.* Toronto: Canadian Institute for International Affairs, 1964.

Natan, Alex, ed. *Swiss Men of Letters.* London: Oswald Wolff, 1970.

Pedrazzini, Mario M. "The Linguistic Problem," in *Switzerland, Present and Future.* Bern: The Yearbook of the New Helvetic Society, 1963, pp. 179-85.

Reverdin, Olivier. *Introducing Switzerland.* Lausanne: Swiss Office for the Development of Trade, 1967.

Rotzler, Willy. "Book Printing in Switzerland," in *Book Typography 1815-1965, in Europe and the United States of America.* London: Ernest Benn, Ltd., 1966, pp. 285-323.

Siegfried, André. *Switzerland: A Democratic Way of Life.* Neuchâtel: La Baconnière, 1950.

Taubert, Sigfred, ed. "Switzerland," in *The Book Trade of the World, Vol. I: Europe and International Section.* Hamburg: Verlag für Buchmarkt-Forschung, 1972, pp. 437-59.

Thürer, Georg. *Free and Swiss.* London: Oswald Wolff, 1970.

SPECIAL STUDIES AND ARTICLES

Béguin, Pierre. "The Press in Switzerland," *Gazette: International Journal for Mass Communication Studies*, No. 2, 1967, pp. 95-102.

SELECTED BIBLIOGRAPHY

Bollinger, Ernst. "Structural Picture of the Swiss Press: Trends and Prospects," *Gazette: International Journal for Mass Communication Studies*, No. 3, 1970, pp. 147-69.

Doka, Carl. "Switzerland's Four National Languages." Zurich: Pro Helvetia, 1970. 11p.

Egger, Eugène. "L'Enseignement en Suisse." Zurich: Pro Helvetia, 1971. 45p.

Gut, Theodor. "Village Voices," *IPI (International Press Institute) Report*, June 1967, pp. 10-11.

Jäger, Josef. "La Presse Suisse." Bern: Schweizerische Politische Korrespondenz, 1967.

Jäger, Josef. "Die Schweizerische Lokalpresse," *Gazette: International Journal for Mass Communication Studies*, No. 2, 1967, pp. 183-94.

Mayer, Kurt. "Cultural Pluralism and Linguistic Equilibrium in Switzerland," *American Sociological Review*, April 1951, pp. 157-63.

Meynaud, Jean. "Le problème des langues dans l'administration fédérale helvétique." Ottawa: Royal Commission on Bilingualism and Biculturalism, 1968. (Unpublished study)

Riesco, Basilio. "Press and Television Advertising in Switzerland," *Gazette: International Journal of Mass Communication Studies*, No. 2, 1967, pp. 161-72.

Thommen, André. "Population: 6,000,000, Languages: 4, Papers: 490," *IPI Report*, June 1967, pp. 8-9.

Uebersax, Peter. "The Logical Step: Go National," *IPI Report*, November 1967, pp. 6-7.

Zinsli, Paul. *Vom Werden und Wesen der mehrsprachigen Schweiz.* Bern: Verlag Feuz, n.d. (Series: Schriften des Deutschschweizerischen Sprachvereins No. 1.) 35p.

In addition to these sources, the official journal of the Swiss Booksellers' and Publishers' Association (*Der Schweizer Buchhandel*, Schweizerischer Buchhändler-und Verleger-Verein, SBVV), provides current articles on book publishing. Published twice a month.

For statistical information: *Annuaire Statistique de la Suisse* (Bern: Bureau Fédéral de Statistique). Published annually.

INDEX

INDEX

INDEX

INDEX

INDEX